DIPLOMATIC IDEAS AND PRACTICES
OF ASIAN STATES

INTERNATIONAL STUDIES
IN
SOCIOLOGY AND SOCIAL ANTHROPOLOGY

General Editor

K. ISHWARAN

VOLUME LIII

ASHOK KAPUR

DIPLOMATIC IDEAS AND PRACTICES OF ASIAN STATES

DIPLOMATIC IDEAS AND PRACTICES OF ASIAN STATES

EDITED BY

ASHOK KAPUR

E.J. BRILL
LEIDEN • NEW YORK • KØBENHAVN • KÖLN
1990

The preparation of the index was supported by a Canadian Social Sciences and Humanities Council grant.

Library of Congress Cataloging-in-Publication Data

Diplomatic ideas and practices of Asian states/edited by Ashok Kapur.
p. cm.—(International studies in sociology and social anthropology, ISSN 0074-8684: v. 53)
ISBN 90-04-09289-7
1. Asia—Foreign relations. I. Kapur, Ashok. II. Series.
JX1569.D56 1990
327'.095—dc20

80-2065
CIP

ISSN 0074-8684
ISBN 90 04 09289 7

PRINTED IN THE NETHERLANDS

CONTENTS

Preface

ASHOK KAPUR

THIS COLLECTION OF PAPERS was inspired by two considerations. First, the Asian geostrategic arena has emerged as the centre of international change and conflict in the post-war era. Comparatively, European international relations and US-USSR relations as they relate to arms control, European security and Third World conflict issues are in a stable and a predictable phase. Here the post-Cold War approach has been to adjust East-West power relationships without disturbing the territorial status quo in Europe and to conduct foreign policy according to the classical European principles of compromise and compensation among the powers. In contrast, power relations in the Asian and the Indian Ocean arena are fluid; the structures of power in the Asian continent, in regional security systems and in the Pacific and Indian Oceans are evolving and they are not easy to categorise. The internal and external imperatives of major Asian powers are varied and changing as are the internal and external power relationships among Asian states; and the mental outlooks of Asian political leaders are also varied. Japan has arrived as an economic superpower on the world scene and is gradually developing its presence in the Asian/Pacific/Indian Ocean arena. This arena remains a flashpoint of superpower naval and air confrontation especially in the North Pacific. The Peoples Republic of China has turned its back against Maoism and Marxism. Its future as an Asian power is assured but the range and limit of its diplomatic skill and its economic and military prowess is still unclear. Australia is slowly developing the Asian dimension of its diplomacy recognising the limitations of its Western contacts but it must work in the context of a growing anti-nuclear sentiment in the South Pacific and a complicated international environment. The international relations of Southeast Asia appear to be on a steady course. There are signs that the interventionist impulses of extra-regional powers have been sharply curtailed, and the danger of Vietnamese domination has also been checked. However, the South Asian and Gulf regions remain the centres of gravity of militarisation and war, ethnic conflict, internal political challenges and regime change and shaky diplomatic dialogues among hostile pairs of states. Thus, a stable Europe and a steady superpower relationship on the one hand and a turbulent and changing Asian/Gulf arena on the other hand, is the setting for this collection of essays on Asian diplomatic and military affairs.

Secondly, at a time when the Asian/Pacific/Indian Ocean arenas are growing in importance in the economic, military, diplomatic and social spheres, the academic literature, especially in North America, is failing to stay abreast of modern developments and to provide the necessary data and theoretical guidance. Here the danger is that such neglect will fail to provide the academic infrastructure which is requited to prepare our students to cope with Asian international relations, and which is needed by academicians and practitioners to make intelligent policies and to shape modern political thought. The premise is that comparative study of Asian diplomatic theories and practices is required to fulfil academic and policy tasks.

The present volume is a step in this direction but I am aware of the limitations. The coverage is not comprehensive, partly because of limited space and partly because of a shortage of available expertise. My hope is that readers will share their criticisms and constructive suggestions for improvement with the editor so as to build on this modest effort.

Introduction: An Overview of Asia

ASHOK KAPUR

THE IDEA OF ASIA was created by Europeans, for Europeans and it led to Western dominance of vast lands and of large numbers of peoples who possessed tremendous wealth and a sense of history and culture. This idea passed through several hands. A number of attitudes and policies emerged as a result, each representing the practical circumstances of the makers of Asia. The Greeks were the first to conceive the notion of Asia. To them the Aegean sea was the centre of the world. The west of Greece was Europe and modern day Turkey and Syria were Asia. The Macedonian expansion brought the Greeks into contact with India. This encounter was brief but it was benign, leading to diplomatic and cultural contact between the two. As a result the Greek idea of Asia was broadened somewhat. The Roman conquests and trade extended the idea of Asia further by its contact with China. Among Asians there was no sense of the Asian collectivity but there was a vague awareness of worlds beyond the princely realms. Thus Indian kings had contact with Persia and China and Indian coastal trade connected the littoral regions of the modern Indian Ocean area. The Chinese empires divided the world between China as the central kingdom and the world of the barbarians. With this in mind an office of Barbarian Affairs was maintained to regulate the contact with foreigners. Invariably the conceptions of these kingdoms were geographically limited and psychologically ethnocentric.[1]

In historic terms the Western dominance of Asia was initiated by the encounter between Christian European and Muslim powers. In this encounter religious, commercial and strategic interests were at work. Seapower played a crucial role in this historic Christian-Muslim fight. Seapower had two qualities: sea transport facilitated trade between Europe and the East; and seapower enabled the projection of superior European sea-based power against Muslim powers and the pagans. Between 1492 and the 1700s (for example the famous Battle of Plassey) the European motive changed from trade to conquest. By the mid 1800s Europeans saw themselves as the superior civilisation and the superior military force. This was a significant reversal of the earlier European view of Asians as superior civilisations.[2]

There was another dimension to the process of Western expansion against Muslims and the pagans. The trade and conquests of Europeans in the Arab,

African, Persian and Asian worlds were driven also by inter-European balance of power struggles. Asian colonialism was a manifestation of the struggle among the powers in Europe, and sea battles between British and French naval forces in the Indian Ocean were signs of intense European rivalries. The encounters among the Europeans in the Afro-Asian-Middle East worlds, and between European powers and powers in these areas, led to a proliferation of dominant-subordinate relations between the metropolitan powers and the colonies. This massive incorporation of third world societies, economies and princely and feudal regimes within the Europe-dominated international system for almost 300 years was a historic development; in contrast the American and the Soviet spheres of influence pale into insignificance. The Soviet empire in Eastern Europe lasted about 40 years; the American century has had a span of about 40 years as well.

Thus, European colonisation served several ends of the European powers. They disoriented third world societies and produced a loss of self-confidence over their inability to meet foreign military and cultural challenges. They brought them under their military and political authority. They organised a transfer of third world wealth into Europe. Finally, they used colonies to transfer European balance of power struggles away from Europe into far-away lands and to regulate their competition and to carry on with balance of power activities as the way to run the system of states. Here the key players were the European powers and the objects or the pawns were Asian polities and societies.

In other words, two main fights brought the Europeans into Asia: (1) the fight between Christian European powers and Muslim powers; and (2) the fight among the European powers for Asian (and third world) spoils on the principle that there had to be a continuous accomodation of the interests of the major players on the basis of compromise and compensation. (Thus, when England got Egypt, it was glad to acknowledge the necessity for France to get Morocco.) By the 19th century a third fight entered the Asian/Middle Eastern picture. After the defeat of the Ottomans and the Muslims by the European powers in the First World War, and after the consolidation of European empires in Asia and other parts of the third world, British fear of Russian expansion and colonisation of Central Asia and its drive towards the Pacific transformed the orientation of the British empire (especially the British India empire) and made the Middle East, South Asia and the Far East the centres of Anglo-Russian rivalry. Asia became the arena in the fight between two highly motivated imperialisms. It became the arena where British policy was quite successful in securing buffers, neutrals and spheres of influence as methods to manage the Russian threat and to organise the frontiers of British and Russian power.[3]

This struggle was still on when a number of events changed the Great Game. (1) European powers became preoccupied with the ideological passions and divisions of fascism, democracy and socialism and with the total war preparations which accompanied the upheavals of the inter-war period. (2)

Japan, a modern industrial and a military power by the turn of the century, defeated Russia in war, and through its challenge to world order and European hegemony of world affairs by its actions in Manchuria, Japan emerged as the first important agent of Pan-Asianism (in Asian eyes) and the first major outsider to move the world towards the Second World War. (3) Russia, a great European power, became weak and corrupt. The Bolshevik revolution changed the power structure in Russia and furthermore, signalled to Asians the possibility that a backward society could change the structure of power if the ruling class lost its will to rule and the lower classes chose to revolt. (4) British imperial authorities realised that British seapower, which had functioned as the backbone of the Empire, could not engage German power which was land-based. During the First World War, London emphasised the utility of Indian manpower in its fight with Germany. The British India empire became the strategic base in the British-German fight, as well as the base for Middle Eastern defence in the 1914-1945 period. Note here that the British strategic compulsion centred on its assessment of the German problem. It lay in a recognition that British capacity to balance power in Europe was at stake. British imperial authority was under attack: from Russians in Central Asia; from the Japanese in Asia when Japanese forces overran British colonies and reached the gates of India; and from Germany in Europe. The growth of Indian nationalism occurred in this historic context. It was a product of British compulsions. Although Indian nationalism possessed a vital indigenous content, it must be admitted that the rise of Gandhi and Nehru on the Indian political scene was facilitated by the emerging structural weaknesses of British power on the world stage before 1945.

The Second World War changed dramatically the Asian scene. In 1945 the structure of world power relations changed significantly and this affected Asia's place in world affairs and the impact of the West on Asia. In 1945 the European powers, including the allies and the victors, lay prostrate in economic and military affairs as a result of the devastation of the war. The superpowers emerged and they came to occupy the centre stage of European affairs. Furthermore, de-colonisation started a process of unravelling of European empires and the rise of new states. The post-war environment carried two meanings. (1) The superpowers emerged as the successors to the European powers in Europe. As the number of key players declined from the usual four or five powers involved in European balance of power activities to two superpowers, and as neither America nor Soviet Russia could alone dominate European or world affairs, the superpowers' competition became bipolarised but interestingly enough the entire globe did not become bipolarised; the superpowers lacked even then the inclination or the capacity to integrate the entire world into their respective military and economic networks. (2) The superpowers did not replace the European powers in Asia except in Japan (which came under exclusive U.S. influence) and Korea where both superpowers divided the peninsula into their respective spheres of influence and bipolarised Korean affairs. In the rest of Asia, especially in China and India, there was much undistributed power (potential economic and military strength and a will towards autonomy) which was outside American and/or Soviet control.[4] Asian nationalism and Asian communism lay behind the drive to organise the undistributed power into autonomous centres of power in Asia which organised power relations in important parts of Asia. This drive enabled these power centres to exploit the superpowers and the international economic and military environment; and to re-define the power relations in the military, economic, diplomatic and cultural spheres among Asian powers and between Asian powers and the powers in the international system. Asian international relations today is a continuing saga along these lines.

Asia is out of the control of the superpowers but Asians see their respective societies and their power relations with the outside world in a process of evolution and transition. The theme in Asian life is captured by the notion of 'restructuring', i.e., a continuous and an extended process of fundamental internal and external change on a number of scales.

(A) *Cultural values*: a struggle between tribal, ethnic, regionalist loyalties and 'national ones'.

(B) *Economic development*: a movement from poverty and disoriented economic activity as a result of colonialism, to an ability to organise internal productive processes and to compete on the world stage, and to develop mutually fruitful exchange relations in lieu of dominant-exploitative relations.

(C) *Political development*: a struggle between feudalism, warlordism and personalised patron-client transactional relations and, on the other hand, the development of institutions and processes to mobilise and organise mass politics and political pluralism.

(D) *Military development*: a movement from a condition of vulnerability to foreign military intervention to a condition of having the capacity and the will to escape forcible intervention and to develop means to project power into the regional neighbourhood and on the world stage.

(E) *Foreign policy development*: a movement from a status of a pawn in the Great powers rivalries (i.e. European rivalries in Asia; superpower and communist states' rivalries in Asia), to an ability to play different roles in the international system from a position of military and economic weakness. Four such roles are noteworthy viz. (i) to function as a bridge builder in East-West affairs (e.g. Nehru in the late 1940s and early 1950s); (ii) to exploit both superpowers for one's own advantage (e.g. Nehru, Chou-en-Lai and most third world countries); (iii) to be isolationist (e.g. Burma); and (iv) to seek an increase in international tension and polarisation between the superpowers so that if the two fight, the weaker party may benefit from the struggle (e.g. Mao and Sun Tzu).

In the context of this massive, all-Asian context of transition and restructuring, the foreign policies of Asian states, generally speaking, may be studied as a continual process to develop temporary alliances with the Great powers. The aim is to exploit the alliance ties for varied purposes: to enhance regime security and/or national security; to achieve internal economic and military development; and to revise power relations with the powers. Here de-colonisation should be studied as an on-going process to re-structure internal power relations within Asian states and societies, to re-structure power relations between hostile pairs of Asian states and among other Asian states, and finally, to restructure the power relations between the major regional powers in Asia and the non-Asian powers. Otherwise, to define de-colonisation as simply a process which ends with the granting of political independence is to trivialise de-colonisation, non-alignment and the third world.

In the first half of this century Asians were attracted to the idea of Pan-Asianism. The development and projection of Japanese power at the turn of the century and in the Second World War revealed this idea. Nehru and his Asian colleagues too pushed this idea in their speeches and in their international conference diplomacy including the Asian Relations conference and the Bandung meeting. This volume realistically rejects the premise of Pan-Asianism as the basis of Asian international relations. The papers deal with a divided Asia because even as Asians face common development problems, their strategic outlooks and interests vary, as do the patterns of their alignment with non-Asian powers in economic, military and diplomatic affairs. Asia is home to practically all major world religions which all speak the language of tolerance, harmony and truth. Yet the combination of religion and politics has contributed to social and military conflict and furthermore, it has made *sub-nationalism* or rather competing sub-nationalisms an elemental force compared to nationalism and communism. As a vital driving element sub-nationalism in Asian politics and international relations merits study but it is outside the scope of this volume.

The papers presented here are a modest attempt to study the agenda and to outline the diplomatic ideas and practices which are in play in Asian affairs. The road to convert the idea of Asia into Asian realities has been a long one. Asian today is not what the Greeks and the Europeans planned or imagined. Asians themselves today do not have a unified conception of what Asia should look like. Nor do I think that it is necessary to have Asia develop a single collective personality or approach to development and security issues. Like the proverbial blind men pronouncing the nature of the elephant by touching parts of it, American, Soviet, Chinese, Japanese, Australian, Indian, Indonesian and other views of the Asian realities will vary. This is just as well since Asian realities are diversified and different ideas enrich the Asian dimension in world affairs. My expectation is not that Asian academic debates will produce a unified Asia but that the increasing presence of Asian states and peoples on the world stage is likely to have a positive effect in connecting Asian realities to world affairs. Out of Asian pluralism in diplomatic and military affairs will come conceptions of regional and international security which reveal the vitality of 'Asian' thinking and which challenge the intellectual and strategic hegemony of the superpowers. Asia today is a vital engine of the third world's revolt against Western (American and Soviet) dominance. If the present pattern of decline of the international authority of the superpowers in different regions in the world is to be understood as a historical process, then the place of Asia in this process and in the future of international relations requires a better understanding. This volume is a modest contribution to this objective.

NOTES

1 C. P. Fitzgerald, "Pan-Asianism," in Guy Wint, ed., *Asia: A Handbook*. Praeger, New York, 1966, pp. 397-99. K. M. Panikkar, *Asia and Western Dominance*. George Allen and Unwin, London, 1959 edition, Introduction.

2 G. Stoessinger, *Nations in Darkness*, Random House, New York, 3rd edition, 1981. P. Mason, *The Men Who Ruled India*, Pan Books, London, 1985, abridged edition.

3 M. Wight, *Power Politics*, Penguin, U.K., 1979, p. 56. Sir Olaf Caroe, *Wells of Power*, MacMillan, London, 1951. Lord Curzon's imperial policy was embedded in this historic British-Russian rivalry.

4 O. Lattimore, *The Situation in Asia*, Little Brown and Co., Boston, 1949. S. S. Harrison, *The Widening Gulf*, Free Press, New York, 1978, part 2.

Iran and Afghanistan: With Specific Reference to Their Asian Policies and Practices*

MIRON REZUN**

ABSTRACT

This article deals with Iran's and Afghanistan's political economic imperatives as part of a medium power's diplomatic theory and practices. It traces the philosophical precepts behind the Shah's and Khomeini's political creed and details the dynamics of conflictive and diplomatic interactions of Iran and Afghanistan with Moslem Arab and Moslem non-Arab states in southwest Asia. An attempt is also made to link these two countries with other countries in Asia such as China, through a modern railway construction in an effort to draw the area more closely into an Asian economic infrastructure. The author concludes that the Iranian experience in diplomacy is a unique one, much more so than that of Afghanistan, although Iran, too, may be tilting further to the USSR.***

COMMENTATORS ON INTERNATIONAL RELATIONS often regard diplomatic theories and practices of smaller nations as a function of superpower rivalry. They see these states as influenced by, or subservient to, the superpower(s). This approach is not entirely valid. A case can be made for examining the policies and attitudes and the inherent imperatives that drive an Asian state or a medium power to behave the way it does. Here a country's diplomatic theory and practice is understood not in terms of the role assigned to it by the superpowers; it is better understood in terms of the country's imperatives, of which superpower rivalry is one element. Foreign conduct has never been an entirely discretionary activity, and it has never entirely been defined as a reflection of the dictates of an allied power. Iran and Afghanistan are two countries which best illustrate these characteristics, particularly in their relations with other Asian countries.

Iran and Afghanistan are located on the periphery of South Asia and Soviet Central Asia. Despite changing internal and external circumstances in both countries since 1978-79, several qualities distinguish these countries. Both are non-Arab Moslem states; both have a common history; both are located in a strategically volatile region; both have some similarity in the ethnic and

* This is part of a project dealing with the USSR and its southern periphery. I am grateful to the Social Sciences and Humanities Research Council of Canada for its generous financial support.

** Department of Political Science, University of New Brunswick, Fredericton, Canada.

*** Parts of this article were adapted from a book edited by Miron Rezun, *Iran at the Crossroads*, Westview Press, Boulder and London, 1990.

racial composition of their populations; and both are territorially contiguous to the USSR on their northern frontiers and with South Asia in the east.

We already know that in the well-publicized "Great Game" of Asia, Iran and Afghanistan were, and still are, the regions most coveted by the principal actors—the Western powers and Russia.[1] Can we not now investigate the extent to which both Iran and Afghanistan have been policy-makers in their own right, if such has been the case at any given time? The most fitting framework for this would involve a discussion of Iran and Afghanistan in terms of: a) the changing ideologies, b) the geopolitics of the region, 3) the correlation of forces. In the opinion of this writer this is the only possible approach; otherwise the pages that follow will result in a mere treatment of the countries' respective ideologies and in the usual monotony of excessive speculation about the future of Afghanistan after the withdrawal of Soviet troops and the prospects for Iran now that the Ayatollah Khomeini has passed from the scene.

Imperial Iran

Let us begin with Iran. The land of Zoroaster had been conquered by the Arab Moslems in the seventh century. When the Pahlavi monarchy was established, its leading intellectuals never really forgot the nation's pre-Islamic past. Pahlavism made official a national mythology that began in the nineteenth century under a weaker Qajar rule. It was vigorous nationalism aimed to glorify the pre-Islamic past and Iranian kingship dating from the fifth century B.C. Its high point was reached in the celebration of 2,500 years of monarchy at Persepolis in 1971. By regenerating dynastic rule it rejected of course, any idea of Islamic ideology from the moment the first Pahlavi monarch, Reza Shah, ascended the Persian throne in 1925.

The architect of this secular, nationalist society, was not really Reza Shah however;[2] rather, it was a man who helped put Reza on the throne and conducted the diplomacy of the nation by himself—Reza's Minister of the Court, Teymourtash.[3] Teymourtash and the triumvirate he headed had Iranian history rewritten to play down the Islamic period. A nationalist campaign was promoted to galvanize the support of the Iranian people beyond the intellectual strata, evoking and emphasizing an Aryan civilization since antiquity (*Iran - e - Bastan*) and a purity of the Persian language (*FARSI-ye ser*ᶜ*e*) which set Iran apart from its immediate neighbours, both Arab and non-Arab, but particularly the Arabs whom Iranian leaders regarded as "barbarian" (*Vahshigari arab*). These invocations were one of the reasons behind a desire for expansionism and territorial aggrandizement.

One notable incident took place at the time King Amnanullah of Afghanistan was deposed in 1929 on a surge of Moslem fundamentalism. Teymourtash in fact sent a whole army to the Afghan border in a bid to seize the Afghan province of Herat in a moment of Afghan weakness.[4] Mutual accommodations between Iran and Afghanistan followed only after Soviet and Turkish mediation. But similar territorial claims were made in this period on

Bahrein and on territories in the Persian Gulf perceived to be inhabited by Arabs of Persian stock. Claims to Soviet territory—particularly to Soviet Azerbaijan and parts of Central Asia—were also made in private to Nazi officials at a time of great sympathy in Iran for the German (Aryan) cause prior to and during World War II.[5]

However, it was not until the advent of Mohammed Reza Shah, Reza Shah's son, that Iran seriously began propagating its age-old national mythology and was able to arrogate to itself a preeminent role in the affairs of the Gulf. In the latter '60s and during the '70s, oil revenues had made Iran a second-ranking power in international politics, the "gendarme" of Persian Gulf security, on a par with such states as India, despite the fact that India supports a population twenty times as large and occupies an area that is only twice as large as Iran's.

Iranian nationalism opposed Arab Nasserism; Iran sent troops to help the Royalists in North Yemen while Nasser helped the Arab nationalists trying to set up a republic. The Shah was able to explain this action by maintaining that Nasserism was heavily influenced and even controlled by Soviet ideological imperatives, though Nasser's entire diplomatic record proved quite the contrary. The Shah's own high-handed, nationalistic commitments compelled him to occupy on November 30, 1971, three tiny, but strategically important, islands in the narrow entrance to the Persian Gulf (Abu Musa and the Tumbs). The Shah did his utmost to influence the Arab rulers of all the Gulf littoral states from Oman to Kuwait, not only because Iran had become the strongest military power in the region, but also because there were more than one million people of Iranian descent living there. The largest military operation in which Iranian forces were involved also took place in 1971, when Iran sent troops to the Sultan of Oman to put down the rebellion in Oman's southern province of Dhofar. The Shah's greatest diplomatic maneuver came even earlier: in 1955 when he adhered to the short-lived Baghdad Pact to form a "Northern Tier" alliance between Iran, Turkey, Pakistan and Iraq (which Great Britain subsequently joined) as a defensive barrier to contain the USSR in the north, a kind of connecting link between NATO in the West and SEATO in the East. But in 1958 Iraq withdrew from the Pact, and from then on it ceased to be called the Baghdad Pact and was renamed CENTO, the Central Treaty Organization, without Baghdad.[6]

This leads us to the most critical issue in Iran's desire to dominate West Asia: its rivalry in the region with Iraq. This rivalry only appeared to end when the Shah and Saddam Hussein signed the Treaty of Algiers in 1975, reaching total agreement on all outstanding disputes. But these disputes, including the border demarcation of the Shat-al-Arab river estuary, were far too deep to lay to rest with the mere stroke of a pen. While the Iran of the Pahlavis was a state purporting to national regeneration, this was not in the least inconsistent with the official religion of this nation, which is Shiᶜite Islam as opposed to Sunni Islam. The leaders of Iran have always been Sunni Moslems ruling an Arab country that is predominantly (more than one-half)

Shi^c^ite. Iran under the Shah was therefore not loath to play on Shi^c^ite sentiments in the diplomatic disputes with Iraq that persisted up to 1975 and which were to reappear more vehemently when the Islamic Republic of Iran was established in 1979.

During the propaganda war between the two countries in the '60s and '70s, Iran identified Iraqi leadership with Yazid—the ruler of Iraq who in the seventh century killed Hossein, the grandson of the prophet Mohammed and one of the founders and martyred heroes of Shi^c^i Islam. It is in Iran's relations with Iran that we clearly see how the ancient animosity between Arabs and Persians is directly transcended by their respective interpretations of Islam. On more than one occasion the Pahlavi monarch was implicated in several unsuccessful coups against the ruling Ba^c^ath regime in Iraq, and this occurred even before Khomeini called for the overthrow of Saddam Hussein.

"My enemy's enemy is my friend" is an old dictum that did not escape the attention of the Pahlavi ruler. Moreover, the reference here is not only to the Iraqi Kurds whom the Shah and the Iranian Government assisted financially and militarily to fight the regime in Baghdad, but also, and more specifically, to the Israelis. This relationship with Israel goes as far back as 1950, (for some, all the way back to the *Book of Esther*) only two years after the establishment of *Eretz Yisrael*, when Iran extended to it a *de facto* recognition. A tacit understanding existed since then, with the implication that Iran was to dominate West Asia while Israel would be supreme in the Middle-East proper. Although this attitude to Israel changed somewhat after the 1967 and the 1973 wars, Imperial Iran never, not even when relations with Egypt improved after 1973, endorsed the idea of a Palestinian state. Countless Iranian officers received training in Israel or had visited that country; both countries exchanged military supplies; and Israel's Mossad and Iran's Savak cooperated in the field of intelligence since 1950 (the Mossad consistently trained Savak operatives). Iran even became Israel's chief supplier of oil. After the 1967 war, Iran financed the Israeli-built 162-mile pipeline from Eilat on the Red Sea to Ashkelon on the Mediterranean.[7]

Apparently Iranian foreign policy of this period was intent not so much on penetrating neighbouring areas as much as it was on influencing them, literally recreating a Persian Empire that only an advanced state like Germany, Britain, or Russia would have attempted, or dared, in previous decades. This is probably one of the most innovative features of the Pahlavi regime. For instance, because the land mass of Western Asia is vast and sparsely populated, Iran entered the old "Great Game" by improving on the rail links of the Indo-Persian corridor, the instrument of land penetration that the Shah hoped would ultimately extend to the vast railway network of former British India. Railways in the developing world are still, after all, the sinews of political and economic penetration. Reza Shah (with the help of German engineers) had been able to complete the 1,400 kilometer-long Trans-Iranian Railway, which is a north-south line. What his son was striving for was an east-west line that would have redirected the flow of Afghan trade away from the

The Indo-Persian Corridor showing projected Iranian railroads

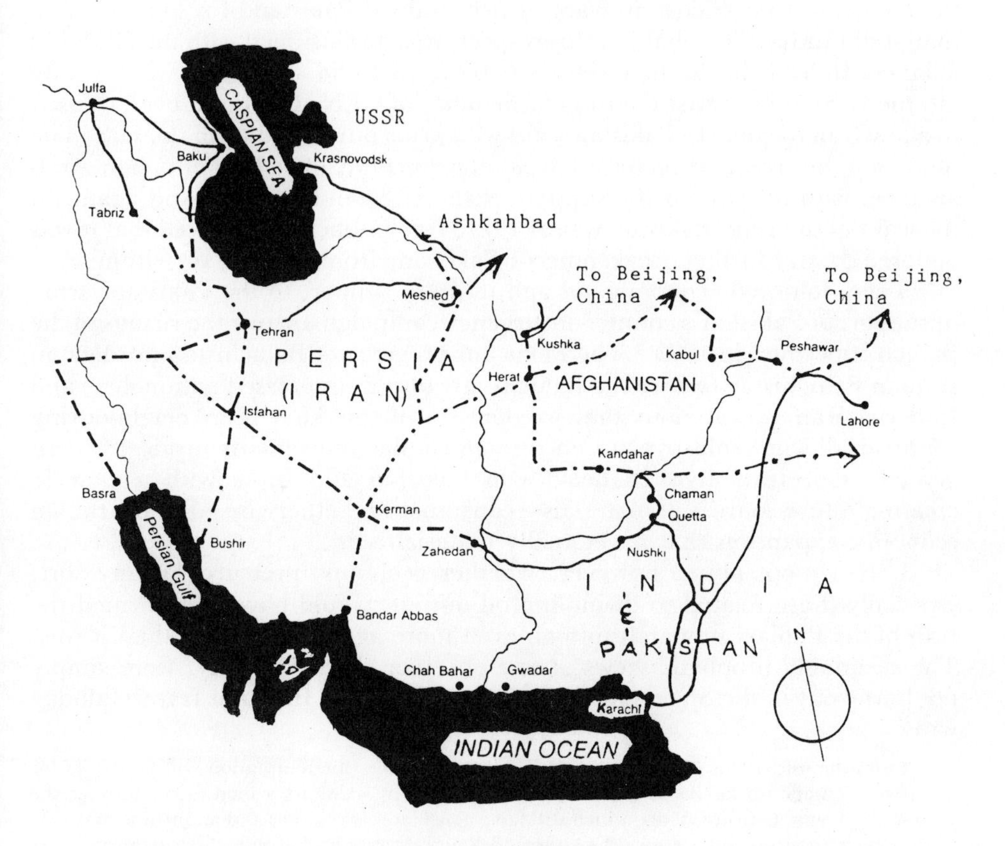

Source: This is the author's impression. See also Milan Hauner, "The USSR and the Indo-Persian Corridor" in *Problems of Communism*, Jan.-Feb., 1987.

Soviet border back to the markets of South Asia and the Middle East. To do this he had to link up the Iranian and Pakistani rail systems. A spur from Qom, passing through Yazd, reached Kerman in 1977. The main Afghan cities—Herat, Kandahar and Kabul—were supposed to be connected to this railroad, and it was thence to be extended to connect with China. The People's Republic of China had just been finishing the 1,200 kilometer-long Karakoram highway crossing the Himalayas from Kashogar to Islamabad.[8] The Iranian dream was thus to establish a Teheran-Kabul-Islamabad (perhaps even a Beijing) axis and project Iranian influence over this new transportation infrastructure, an event of major geostrategic significance for both India and the USSR. For this purpose, the Shah actually gave Afghan President Mohammed Daoud a two billion dollar credit.

If for no other reason this was principally why Iran was so dismayed over the recurring Indo-Pakistani wars, which drained Pakistan of resources more than it did India. The Shah, in this respect, was disillusioned with the CENTO alliance. Indeed, in the first 1965 war between India and Pakistan, not only did the U.S. fail to assist Pakistan (a member of CENTO), but it even refused to allow Iran to come to Pakistan's aid with arms purchased from the U.S. The Shah saw his country increasingly as the linchpin of a Moslem, non-Arab alliance, with or without the support of the U.S. and Britain. And again, in the wake of the Indo-Pakistan war of 1971, Iran publicly announced that it was opposed to any further weakening of Pakistan, from without or within.

There followed economic aid and military support to the Pakistani army in support of Pakistan's counter-insurgency campaign against the risings of the Baluch tribesmen in 1973.[9] The Pakistani province of Baluchistan borders on Iranian Baluchistan (where the Baluchis are also a suppressed nationality) and Imperial Iran was anxious that irredentism of this kind from neighbouring countries did not spill over to encourage similar movements inside Iran. In general, too, Iran invested heavily in Pakistan and India with a view to creating future sources of materials—consumer and otherwise—for an Iranian economic expansion that never really materialized.

It is a moot point, however, whether economic pressures of any sort, especially those related to dwindling oil output, would have transformed the Iran of the Pahlavi monarch into an even more aggressive power than it was. The seemingly prophetic views of one observer, Fred Halliday, were simply not borne out in the Shah's lifetime. Before the fall of Imperial Iran, Halliday wrote:

> From the mid-1980s onwards, as Iran's oil output falls, the temptation will be strong for Iran to make up for the fall in its domestic output by using its armed forces to seize the wells of neighbouring states, which still have considerable reserves and an income in excess of their requirements: Kuwait, Qatar and Saudi Arabia all fall into this category.[10]

But in those days was Iran genuinely the overwhelmingly powerful nation in the region that so many led us to believe? Iran had acquired more military hardware than it could possibly use or even knew how to use. Could not, even then, a combined Arab force still have held its own against a supremely equipped Iranian Army and Navy? For in any case the records eloquently show that the Iranian forces were primarily used to suppress the Iranian people so as to maintain the Pahlavi dynasty in power. Certainly the mantle of would-be Iranian supremacy would fall on Khomeini's Islamic Republic, in much the same way that Soviet Russia inherited many of the features of foreign policy which were characteristic of Tsarist Russia before it, with some notable differences of course.

The Islamic Republic

Not its Indo-European origins, to be sure, but the creed of Ithna 'Ashari Shi'ism constituted that exceptional difference between Khomeini's Iran and

Iran under the Shah. Shiʾis throughout the centuries regard as usurpers al the successors of Mohammad, whether Arab caliphs or Persian and Arab monarchs, recognizing only the descendants of Ali's (Mohammad's cousin and son-in-law) line as the "infallible" and "sinless" Imams. There were twelve such Imams; Khomeini himself is said to be a temporary incarnation of the last Imam, pending the Imam's second coming in the last Day of Judgment as the Mahdi, a Messiah of the world, who will come to redeem the faithful.

In 1501 the Safavid dynasty established a new Iranian state and declared this Ithna ʿAshari form of Shiʾism to be the official religion of the state. But becasue Shiʾi doctrine does not recognize temporal rulers as legitimate, it makes no separation between religion and politics. In this, Khomeini is at one with the founder of the Moslem Brotherhood, Hassan el-Banna, who said "Islam is a home and a nationality, a religion and a state, a spirit and a word, and a book and a sword".

But the Shiʾite perception of that fundamentalism goes even further in its scheme of things. The ideology of the Islamic Republic of Iran has an external as well as an internal dimension, just as do the *Zahir* (exoteric) and *Batin* (esoteric) Shiʾi precepts of this branch of Islam. The internal dimension is rooted in the fact that the Ithna "Ashari Shiʾi" belief postulates that Islam is an impetus for revolution. For centuries the Shiʾite sect of Islam has been the religion of dissent in Iran with the clergy acting as the most vocal opponnents of unpopular monarchs; and because of persecution suffered at the hands of the Sunnis, the concepts of martyrdom deeply ingrained in the Iranian psyche. Externally, Shiʾi Iran is fundamentally anti-Western; it is also exportable to all other Moslem states, primarily to all secular states in the region, whether a pseudo-socialist state like the Baathist regime in Iraq, or the erstwhile military dictatorships using Islam as a pretext, like Pakistan. Khomeini is not only leader of the 100 million Shiʾis in the world: he has been designated by the Ithna ʿAshari Shiʾi theory of government as the leader of all the 800 million Moslems in the world, comprising both Sunnis and Shiʾis. This precept has actually been written into the Constitution of the Islamic Republic. Article 10 of the Constitution reads:

> All Moslems form a single nation, and the Government of the Islamic Republic of Iran has the duty of formulating its general policies with a view to the merging and union of all Moslem peoples, and it must constantly strive to bring about the political, economic and cultural unity of the Islamic world.[11]

In foreign policy, in particular, this theocratic worldview amounts to a rejection of the contemporary international system as it exists. To deal with that system, however, Iran has, as one analyst aptly puts it, brought about "a deliberate transformation of the Major alignments of Iran's foreign relations as they existed previously".[12] According to another observer, Professor Ramazani, Khomeini's worldview is based on six general principles: (a) no dependence on East or West (b) the U.S. is the main enemy (c) struggle against the Zionist power (d) the liberation of Jerusalem (e) anti-imperialism and, most important of all (f) support for all oppressed peoples everywhere, and particularly for Moslems. There is evidently an element of populism, even of socialism, in references to oppressed peoples; and the Soviet Union is of course never depicted as negatively as the United States. While there may be a convergence of views between Iran and the USSR in regard to the "imperialism" of the Western powers, the Soviet Union is not in fact typically "anti-Western", which is patently the case with Iran. Nor will Iran's Shiʾism acknowledge the orthodox Marxist division of the world into socialist and capitalist states; instead, it refers to the traditional Islamic division of the world into *dar al-Islam* (house of Islam) and *dar al-harb* (house of war).

But nowhere does Shiʾism apply more critically than in relation to the Arab states, and to those of the Gulf in particular; in the Iranian mind these states have defected from true Islam. From the very outset, Ayatollah Montazeri, Khomeini's now-deposed religious successor, explained Iran's attitude to other Moslems thus:

> One of the characteristics of Iran's Islamic Revolution is that its mundane scope cannot be confined to certain geographical and continental areas. Indeed, our revolution is an Islamic revolution, not an Iranian revolution ... Final victory will be achieved when there is no trace of colonialism and exploitation left throughout the entire Islamic world... All Muslims and defenceless persons in the world who are living under dictatorship and colonialism have certain expectations from the Muslim nation of Iran, and our glorious revolution is duty-bound toward these people. The Iranian government and people, to the extent they can, must give material and psychological support and assistance to all freedom movements, especially to the Palestinian revolution.[14]

Clearly, these remarks were made in the year of Khomeini's accession to power. In February 1979, Yasir Arafat, leader of the Palestine Liberation Organization had been the first foreign dignitary to officially visit the Islamic Republic. Khomeini's good-will gesture to Arafat was to allow him to expropriate the vacated Israeli embassy in Teheran.

However, when war broke out between Iran and Iraq in September 1980, this astute Palestinian leader suddenly found that he had to choose between his allegiance to the Arab nationalism of Iraq and his sympathy for the Iranian revolution. But few Palestinians (except those rioting against Israeli administration in the Gaza Strip and some on the West Bank) were ever sympathetic to Iranian Shiʾism. Many have, on the contrary, volunteered to fight on the Iraqi side: and it came as no surprise in the end when Arafat abandoned his short-lived alliance with Khomeini. Since then the PLO has been in conflict with all fundamentalist Moslem groups. Khomeini has always realized that Arafat's objective lies in the creation of a secular Palestinian state. In Lebanon, for instance, pro-Khomeini Shiʾi militiamen have been fiercely battlling PLO forces; in early 1985 Shiʾi forces loyal to the Lebanese Hizbʾ Allah (the Party of God) made an aborted attempt to destroy the PLO camps in the Beirut area. Throughout Lebanon Hizbʾ Allah's exploits have included kidnappings of Americans and Europeans, suicide attacks, hijackings (witness the case of the *Air Afrique* jet where a French passenger was murdered in July 1987). The media have recently reported that Khomeini "is said to spend anywhere from $15 million to $50 million a year to finance Hazbʾ Allah activities in Lebanon".[15]

In addition to Lebanon the Iranians are adroitly exploiting their kinship with the Shiʾi minorities of the Gulf Arab states: Kuwait, 30-40 per cent; Dubai, 30 per cent; Qatar, 20 per cent. More important to Teheran are the Gulf states where the Shiʾis constitute one-half of the whole population or where they are an actual majority but living under a Sunni government: Oman, 50 per cent; Iraq, 60 per cent; Bahrein, 75 percent, not to mention Lebanon again where today Shiʾis are more numerous than the Sunni Moslems and the Maronite and Orthodox Christians. To all these Shiʾi elements Iran has made repeated calls to rise in revolt against their "illegitimate" Sunni governments.

The subversive methods Iran employs are the subject of the world's headlines. In some Gulf states agents of the Islamic Republic have set up secret celles known as Hussainiyyas which masquerade as religious study groups; sometimes they go unnoticed escaping the vigilant eye of the local police and sometimes they are detected by the Arab security agencies and suppressed. Iran is already on record for trying to overthrow the Bahrein government in December of 1981, and it is responsible for an abortive group in Qatar in the autumn of 1983. In September of 1982 an Iranian Shiʾi leader, Hujjat Al-Islam Musavi Khuayni, led a group of Shiʾis to Mecca during the ceremonial *Hajj* and publicly announced that his goal was to dispose of the "corrupt" Saudi royal family. A much larger variation on the same theme occurred in the first week of August 1987, when thousands of Iranian pilgrims rioted and attempted to seize the sacred Mosque at Mecca; their aim was to topple the Sunni-ruled kingdom and proclaim Khomeini the leader of all Islam. The bid was foiled by Saudi security forces (possibly with the assistance of U.S. military and naval intelligence) but the event left well over 400 persons dead and Saudi-Iranian relations soured for years to come.

Not surprisingly, the most novel aspect of the Iranian revolution (in addition to the Soviet invasion of Afghanistan of course) is that it inflicted the final blow to CENTO, an alliance—as we observed earlier—about which the Shah had so many misgivings. The threat of an exportable Ithna Ashari Shiʾi led to the establishment in 1981 of the Gulf Co-operation Council (GCC), a kind of collective security belt composed of Saudi Arabia, Bahrein, Oman, Kuwait, Qatar and the United Arab Emirates. The GCC's defense budget is above $40 billion per year, which includes American AWAC planes and other sophisticated military equipment totalling more than half of what the whole Third World earmarks for defense spending. Moreover, this whole outlay was never a deterrent to the Iranian threat; the only state that was concerned over it is Israel, not Iran. Arguably, the only viable deterrent against Iran in the Persian Gulf is the U.S. Rapid Deployment Joint Task Force (RDF) which, since January 1983, has become the U.S. Central Command, or USCENTCOM with a power-projection second only to NATO in Europe.[16]

What is surprising, however, is Iran's relationship with Syria, an Arab country ruled by Moslem Alawites who trace their allegiance to Ismailism, one of the offshoots of the Shi'i movement. The Alawites have had more affinity with the Shi'is in Iran than with Sunni Arabs elsewhere. But Syria is, above all, also a nationalist Arab country ruled by a single-party Baathist regime. Syria's rivalry with Iraq has brought it closer to Iran and, together with Libya, it was the only Arab country supporting the Iranian war effort. But it is wrong to infer—as many analysts have often suggested—that Iran maintains friendly ties only with those Arab countries who belong to the "rejectionist front" in relation to Israel.

In point of fact, Syria is now seen loosening its ties with Iran. Syria after all has had its own problems with Moslem fundamentalists such as the Moslem Brotherhood; why then should Syria want a fundamentalist regime in Iraq in the event of an Iranian victory? The Syrians fought and reportedly cleared the Bekaa Valley of Khomeini supporters[17]—the Hizb'Allah Party—and, by mid-August of 1987, in a conciliatory gesture to the United States, the Syrians helped free the American journalist Charles Glass from his Shi'i kidnappers. This is not to say that Hafez Assad of Syria would suddenly haved changed sides in the Gulf War on grounds of a belated recognition of commitment to the Arab cause. His ties with Iran are above all of a practical nature: Syria receives special concessions on oil purchases in Iran.

The most dramatic impact on Iranian foreign policy was of course the war with Iraq. After eight years this war has already exceeded in casualties all of the Arab-Israeli wars combined, ranking sixth in terms of damage and death among all interstate wars in the world since 1815. Iraq started the conflict with a pre-emptive strike in September 1980 but, again, it came about as a result of Iran's calling on the Shi'is in Iraq to revolt and overthrow the Baath Government and the ruling "*Tekriti*" clique of Saddam Hussein. The Voice of Revolutionary Iran often exhorted the more than five million "sons of Ali to rise up against the sons of Yazid", invocations reminiscent of Iranian propaganda at the time of the Shah. Financial assistance was sent to the *al-Da'wa* underground Shi'i movement in Iraq and in 1980 members of the *al-Da'wa* tried to assassinate Mr. Tariq Aziz, Iraq's future foreign minister. All Arab Gulf States who have been bankrolling Iraq—primarily Saudi Arabia and Kuwait—and those who have sent pilots and arms (Jordan, Egypt) also became the targets of Iran's fury. Thus the war has not been confined to the battle fields along their common border, but has been carried on by proxy to Lebanon, Abu Dhabi, Turkey, Libya and even to Paris and London.

The Saudis and their Arab allies have been coordinating their OPEC oil-price stance at meetings of the Arab League heads of government at which Iran was repeatedly condemned for occupying Iraqi territory.

In a certain sense until now Iran has not had much of a dialogue, nor much of a diplomacy for that matter, with any Arab state except Libya, Algeria and Syria. Its ties with Pakistan are tenuous at best; it tolerates but does not recognize the Soviet-supported Marxist regime in Afghanistan.

Although there are many Shi'ites living in Afghanistan's border region of Herat, the population of Afghanistan is for the most part Sunni. In the eighteenth century the Iranian Safavid dynasty had been temporarily overthrown by an invasion of Afghans who tried to impose Sunnism on Iran—an event that has not been forgotten by the current Shi'i leadership who still regard the Afghan refugees in Iran as third-class citizens. Relations with Afghanistan are nonetheless improving because of the proposed new rail links and because of Afghan manpower in Iran that has freed many able-bodied Iranians for the war. When Soviet troops were finally withdrawn from Afghanistan, Iran played a more important role in Afghan affairs and acquired a new market for its goods. But all this does not mean that the Shi'i regime is by definition incapable of evolution from within and impervious to change from without. Let us examine the evidence.

First, the internal situation in Iran is far from optimistic. There is high inflation: rampant corruption has reached intolerable proportions; food, fuel and electricity are in short supply, and defections and treason in the military are numerous. The general dissatisfaction with the war is obvious, although the Iranian Central Bank has more than $5.1 billion in foreign reserves to finance another war with oil revenues still climbing, which is a good thing, since Iran, the only pariah in the region, can obtain nothing on credit. Second, Iraq's superiority over Iran in military hardware is approximately 5 to 1. Thirdly, there appears to be a fierce power struggle in the Government between moderates and hard-liners. Following the revelations and scandal that erupted in connection with the secret McFarlane mission to Teheran in 1986 and indirect bargaining with the U.S. and Israel for necessary military equipment and spare parts, the more moderate Rafsanjani, on several occasions publicly declared:

> There are at present two relatively powerful factions in our country with differences of view on how the country should be run and on the role of the government and that of the private sector in affairs. These two tendencies also exist in the Majlis, in the government, within the clergy, within the universities and across society as a whole... They may in fact be regarded as two parties without names.[18]

Finally, the very notion—antithetical to the Iranian line thus far—that some secret accommodation might be reached with the U.S. out of sheer necessity, brought Khomeini round to supporting the hard-liners himself in this internal struggle. Not so much fanaticism, to be sure, but an astute example of histrionics is what characterized the Shi'i riots in Mecca in the summer of 1987. No doubt Khomeini mounted this spectacle to deflect public opinion from the internal problems and to help cement the unity of the country. This in effect is the art of crisis management, which now becomes an essential part of Iranian statecraft as well. Propaganda created in the public mind a chronic sense of crisis during the Mecca pilgrimage. Then the state showed its mettle and its determination to rise to the occasion by taking bold and decisive actions (i.e. war games in the Gulf code-named "martyrdom") reflected an element of risk and proving that it will shrink from no danger. According to a prominent Western observer, Gary Sick, "the revolutionary regime in Teheran aspires, as did the Shah before it, to be recognized as the dominant power of the region... Iran's tactical performance has been shrewd and tough. The new regime has used whatever leverage available to seize the initiative and to keep its many adversaries off balance".[19] Interestingly, most other Western commentators, who persistently ignore the relationship between internal conditions in Iran and external actions, seem to believe that when Iran acts pragmatically it acts realistically and adopts a pro-Western and pro-American attitude. This is how Rafsanjani's pro-American lobby is explained. But the only noticeable pragmatism that one is able to detect among the Iranians is the ability to play one power off against another, a constant in the foreign policies of the majority of Asian states who had been subordinated to foreign influences and powers in the past.

Teheran has signed an important trade pact which includes a sizeable arms deal with China for the sale of tanks, planes and "silkworms" missiles and spare parts. Is this not a realistically pragmatic move? Then there is the current friendliness toward Moscow. The turning point came in February 1986 with the arrival in Teheran of Georgi Kornienko (First Deputy Foreign Minister) to begin talks on natural gas deliveries and to establish an Aeroflot route between the Iranian capital and Moscow. That visit was reciprocated by the Iranian Foreign Minister Ali Akbar Velayati to Moscow in February 1987. Amid the upheavals of August 1987, Soviet Deputy Foreign Minister Yuli Vorontsov visited Teheran and asked that Iran stop obstructing the search for a negotiated settlement of the Afghan crisis. He intimated that the USSR, in return, would not support a United Nations resolution that would impose sanctions or a global arms embargo against Iran if Iran failed to observe a ceasefire in the Iran-Iraq war. Considering that only four years ago Iran suppressed the Communist Tudeh Party and jailed or executed the local Communist leaders, this rapprochement with Moscow is most revealing indeed. Warming up to the Soviets would allow Iran to procrastinate on any new U.N. Security Council resolution and Secretary-General Perez de Cuellar's efforts to end the war.[20] The Soviet news agency TASS has repeatedly announced that "Moscow and Teheran are mutually concerned over the unprecedented buildup of the U.S. military presence in the region". And, if anything, Moscow reacted strongly to the Iraqi resumption of the tanker war in the fall of 1987 and has been critical of Iraq ever since.

Strategic imperatives may be of a different order. Iran and the Soviet Union have already begun to reopen oil pipelines, and talks between the two have centered on building a second rail link from Iran to Soviet Central Asia. Because of the Gulf War, Iran has had to expand port facilities at Bandar Abbas and at Shah Bahar. The Islamic Republic has recently taken up the Pahlavi monarch's railway schemes and is interested in establishing a rail link to Bandar Abbas, either from Kerman or Bafq over a distance of roughly 750 kilometers. Work is already moving ahead along the Bam-Shur Gaz alignment towards Zahedan.[21] Again, as in the days of the Shah, (though not for the same reasons) this might be motivated by geostrategic expedience to bring Iran closer to an Asian infrastructure and to Asian markets rather than to the West, thus utilizing to its fullest the advantages of its geographical location. Possibly, too, Iran is turning toward the USSR for another reason: over the past five years Pakistan has been receiving more than $3 million in U.S. military and economic aid, and has become the most important American ally in Southwest Asia. There is some evidence suggesting that the U.S. has or will soon be allowed air bases even in Pakistan's province of Baluchistan and the use of port facilities near Karachi.[22] In this scenario Pakistan could become a significant proxy fighting force in the Gulf, a vital link in the entire USCENTOM defense perimater, a point which further threatens the basic commitments of the Iranian Revolution. These are some of the motivations that eventually prompted Rafsanjani to visit the USSR after Khomeini's death and conclude important arms deals with the Kremlin leaders in the summer of 1989.

Afghanistan

In Afghanistan everything appears to be at once more simple and more complicated that it is in Iran. A far poorer, far less populated and a far less developed country (most of which is both rugged and impenetrable), would suggest at first glance that Afghanistan should not command too much of our attention. But, like Iran, it represents a vast strategic land bridge between East and West and on the strength of that alone it makes for a separate examination, particularly in relation to the unstable politics of the entire region. Yet, unlike Iran, there are two interlocking features that have made both the theory and the practice of Afghanistan's foreign relations less independent as well. First, because of its relative backwardness, Afghanistan has never had a tradition of central government control and administration and, secondly, although the country had never been a colony of any of the imperial powers, Afghan foreign policies have largely been determined by Soviet Russia, not by the internal politics of Afghanistan—except of course where the domestic scene provides alternative, recalcitrant behavior not officially condoned by Kabul, the capital.

For this is a country that defies any attempts at unity. The Kabul authorities have never been able to collect taxes in the countryside, let alone impose any sort of order on the villages. It is probably one of the remaining feudal systems in the world; peasants rarely see the world except in terms defined by strict tribal loyalties. Many languages are spoken: Pushu, Tadzhik, Dari, Farsi, Baluch, Uzbek, Turkoman and so on; the dominant tribal group is the Pathan, or Pushtun—which is also the most volatile. If anything, rural areas are strongly bound and influenced by a rigid Moslem fundamentalism. In this kind of atmosphere it is not uncommon for kingship, which is traditionally of the Durani line and belonging to the Pathan community, to find it exceedingly difficult to manage the rest of such an anarchic state.

Amanullah Khan, the Afghan King, the first Third World ruler to recognize the Soviet Union and conclude a Treaty of Friendship with it in 1921, did his utmost to modernize his country and transform it into a totally secular nation. But Amanullah was neither a Reza Shah of Iran nor the unbending Kemal Ataturk of Turkey; his anti-clericalism was to bring him down in 1929 as the result of a Pushtun uprising that was not without instigation and support from British India. There were many in Afghanistan who felt that, since Ottoman Turkey had ceased to exist and Iran was also departing from its Moslem values under the Pahlavi dynasty, it was up to the Afghan Government to consider itself heir to the Caliphate. Still, the central authorities in Kabul always perceived themselves as being under the influence of the northern neighbour, with a distinct Asian world view. Early in May 1921, Lenin was to write to Amanullah conveying his "sympathy and confidence that no one will encroach on the independence of the High Afghan State either by force or by cunning".[23] Possibly to conciliate the USSR, Afghanistan did not join the League of Nations until the Soviets did in the early thirties. In order not to antagonize the Russians, Kabul joined neither the Baghdad Pact/nor the CENTO "Northern Tier" Alliance aimed at the USSR; Kabul consistently remained neutral and non-aligned, whereas Pakistan remained more important to this alliance from 1954 onward.

It was on January 20, 1955, that Afghanistan established formal diplomatic relations with China. But in China's conflict with India, Afghanistan displayed more sympathy with the latter, all the more so because of a lingering dispute between Pakistan and Afghanistan over "Pushtunistan". From the very outset the Soviets supported Afghan's claims for a greater Pushtunistan, which also included the incorporation of Pakistan's province of Baluchistan into Afghanistan. A Soviet-dominated Baluchistan in Pakistan is a strategic asset: it sits astride the entrance to the Persian Gulf. Since Pakistan began closing its borders to Afghan transit, Afghanistan's land-locked economy became increasingly more dependent on the USSR and on Iran for an outlet for its foreign trade. And since Afghanistan was at loggerheads with Iran over boundaries and water rights in the south-west, the Soviet Union became Afghanistan's major partner. Prime Minister Mohammad Daoud received the lion's share of economic assistance from Moscow, everything from mining development, irrigation projects, oil exploration, roads, airports; in a word, Afghanistan by 1973 had fallen entirely within the Soviet sphere of influence. When in that year Daoud seized power from his cousin King Zahir Shah, the coup was successful only because it was planned and organized by the Parchamite wing of the Marxist People's Democratic wing of the Democratic Party of Afghanistan (PDPA), which has been consistently pro-Soviet. The Parcham leaders in the past held four government ministries.

But in the mid-seventies Daoud (by then King of Afghanistan) came increasingly under the sway of the Shah of Iran who was eager to expand his power across the entire region. The shah was soon offering even more aid than the USSR in areas such as railway construction, water-sharing and mining. He allowed the Iranian SAVAK to infiltrate the country to stamp out both religious conservatism and Marxism; he arrested the leaders of the Khalq and Parcham wings of the Communist Party, and this brought on the coup of April 1978 and brought the Marxist to power. As one of the most informed analysts of the region has pointedly observed: "Put in perspective, the 1978 Afghan coup emerges as one of the more disastrous legacies of the Shah's ambitious effort to roll back Soviet influence in surrounding countries and create a modern version of the ancient Persian empire".[24]

When the Soviets finally arrived in Afghanistan in force to shore up a weak and tottering regime it was mainly in response to China, Pakistan and Iran (not to mention the U.S.) which had been rendering material support to the tribal insurgents. The victory of Moslem fundamentalism in Iran in February 1979 and the overthrow of the Shah had given a powerful boost to Moslem fundamentalism in Afghanistan. Khomeini repeatedly denounced the new Marxist regime, grudgingly accepting many Afghan refugees, but allowing Pakistan to absorb the majority of roughly five million. From the start of the Soviet invasion it was clear that Afghan policies were made in tandem with Soviet policies, although there is ample evidence that Moscow cannot have been too happy with the internal dissensions within the PDPA. The Parcham—which made the decisions and which was always pro-Soviet—was largely composed of Dari-speaking intellectuals; whereas the Khalqi (Masses) were dominated by Pushtun speakers from areas in the East and the South.

The Afghan Communists' greatest mistake has been their headstrong attempts at social transformation and land reform. It was not until the Parchamite, Babrak Karmal, was replaced in May 1986 by the secret police chief Najibullah that intra-party rivalry eventually subsided. Nevertheless, Afghanistan never did have much of a viable diplomacy as long as the war continued.

For their part the partisans themselves offered little in the way of a viable alternative: when not assisted by adventurers and mercenaries, of foreign money and equipment, or Soviet defectors, they were and are still led by a half-dozen, half-baked, rival leaders who are predominantly Sunni Moslems. Their only bond is that they are opposed to both the Soviets and the Communists, with no love lost for the regime in Pakistan. The largest group is led by Rabbani's *Jamiat-i-Islami* Party; the second largest, with a Khomeinist ethic, is Gulbudin Hekmatiar's *Hizbe-i-Islami* and so on. They coalesced in 1986 to form a broad front called the "Islamic Unity of Afghan Mujahideen", claiming to be the legal Government-in-exile and sending both delegations and leaders to Washington for arms and to the United Nations to protest against the official Afghan representatives from Kabul. These partisan groups generally look for support to Pakistan which has encouraged their campaigning and activities in Peshawar, and to China as well, which is linked to Pakistan in an alliance that is essentially a counterpose to India.

After the Soviet invasion of Afghanistan, the ASEAN[25] states took an active part—far more than India—in the diplomatic offensive against the USSR. And China's voice, of course, drowned all the rest. Interestingly though, since Gorbachev's arrival and Soviet shifts in foreign policy, both China and the ASEAN states have muted their criticism of the Soviet presence in Afghanistan; and no positive remarks are now ever made about the sacrifices of the Afghan rebels.

Concluding Remarks

Political scientists are trained to examine patterns and consistencies as well as to recognize anomalies and inconsistencies. All too often, however, informed commentators refuse to recognize the Asian dimensions of Iran's or Afghanistan's foreign policy orientation. American "think tanks" and edited books which discuss the approaches and diplomatic methods of these states have invariably acted as instruments of a Western policy orientation, fulfilling a political (chiefly American) agenda in a conspicuously tendentious manner. In short, we do not objectively analyze the policies of these countries but arrogantly offer prescriptions on how best to deal with, or counter, the alleged psychopathology of such nations in relation only to ourselves in the West.

From what has been said above it becomes patently obvious that Iran has had a far greater influence on the politics of the region than Afghanistan. This is a major consistency that changes little with any change of regime in Iran. The anomaly is that the attitudes of the Iranian nation completely change in distinction to the philosophical foundation of the previous regime. These attitudes evolve to a point where a whole nation can be rationally (or irrationally) mobilized at the behest of a theocratic order. But Iran has more or less always been an independent actor; Afghanistan has not. A deal has now been reached for a gradual Soviet military withdrawal. But what this will spell our for the future of governance in Afghanistan is anyone's guess. Part of that solution will most likely go through the United Nations, where only Afghanistan and Pakistan have been holding proximity sessions since 1982, or by another secret Soviet-American agreement which would enable these U.N.-sponsored negotiations to work out a temporary solution. Not long ago there were proposals to bring together representatives of various factions, including the resistance leaders, some businessmen and a few Communists who would share power under the former King Zahir Shah. Yet it is still hard to estimate if the Soviets could realistically abandon the Afghan Communists, co-opt them into a coalition and at the same time leave them to unruly Moslem tribesmen who, having fought the Soviet presence, will now probably continue fighting amongst themselves.

On the other hand Iran had assured Pakistan that it would not delay a Soviet withdrawal from Afghanistan. But the Iranians obviously want more say in these matters. In fact, in talks held in Teheran, the Iranians told the Soviets that they were opposed to a Zahir Shah solution in view of the King's similarity to the former Shah of Iran. Here again we see a curious mix of both pragmatism and ideological retrenchment in Iranian diplomacy, which has been a consistent practice of Teheran so far. If Gorbachev is now responsible for the withdrawal of Soviet troops from Afghanistan, there is still no evidence that Moscow also wishes to relinquish its political authority in that country. By contrast, the Iranian posture in international affairs will undoubtedly continue for many years.

NOTES

1 For a more recent analysis of the "Great Game" see Miron Rezun, "the Great Game Revisited" in the *International Journal*, vol. XLI., No. 2, Spring 1986, pp. 324-342.

2 Reza Shah was basically illiterate and spent most of his time grooming an army, suppressing internal disorders and appropriating feudal estates.

3 For a full account of Teymourtash, see Miron Rezun, "Reza Shah's Court Minister: Teymourtash" in *International Journal of Middle Eastern Studies*, Los Angeles, No. 12, 1980, pp. 119-137. See also Miron Rezun, *The Soviet Union and Iran*. Sijthoff, Leiden, The Netherlands. 1981, 500 pp. This book has been reissued by Westview Press, Boulder, Colorado, 1988.

4 Miron Rezun, *Op. cit.*, p. 139-140.

5 *Ibid.* See the last chapter in this book. See also Miron Rezun, *The Iranian Crisis of 1941*, Böhlau Verlag, Vienna/Cologne, 1982.

6 The forerunner of the Baghdad Pact was the Saadabad Pact of 1937, in which the Arabs were not represented at all, though at the time Iraq (Mesopotamia) was a British protectorate.

7 Fred Halliday, *Iran, Dictatorship and Development*. Penguin Books, Middlesex, England 1979, p. 279.

8 Milan Hauner, "The USSR and the Indo-Persian Corridor", in *Problems of Communism*, Jan-Feb. 1987, pp. 29-30.

9 Iran sent more than thirty Chinook Helicopter gunships to the Pakistani armed forces, including logistic support.

10 Fred Halliday, *op. cit.*, p. 269.

11 Hamid Algar, (trans.), *Constitution of the Islamic Republic of Iran*. Mizan Press, Berkeley, 1980, p. 31.

12 W. G. Milllward, "The Principles of Foreign Policy and the Vision of World Order expounded by Imam Khomeini and the Islamic Republic of Iran", in Nikki R. Keddie and Eric Hooglund, (eds.) *The Iranian Revolution and the Islamic Republic*, Yale University Press, Washington, D.C. 1982, p. 189.

13 R. K. Ramazani, "Khomeini's Islam in Iran's Foreign Policy", in Dawisha, K. (ed.), *Islam in Foreign Policy*, p. 21.

14 *Iran Voice*, September 3, 1979, p. 1.

15 *Time*, August 17, 1987.

16 CENTCOM is considered to be on a par with NATO in Europe and with CINPAC in the Pacific. It can land an intervention force of 300,000 troops in Southwest Asia, 450,000 by 1989. Lawrence Lifschultz, "From the U-2 to the P-3: The U.S.-Pakistan Relationship", in *Scanner*, Washington, No. 159, Sept/Oct. 1986, p. 72.

17 At one time Menahem Begin of Israel had actually been supplying arms to the Iranian Revolutionary Guards in the Bekaa Valley of Lebanon.

18 FBIS: South Asia, June 11, 1986. Cited by Gary Sick, "Iran's Quest for Superpower Status" in *Foreign Affairs*, Spring, 1987, Vol. 65, No. 4, p. 704.

19 *Ibid.*, p. 713.

20 U.N. Security Council Resolution 598 adopted on July 20, 1987, calls for a ceasefire, exchange of prisoners and withdrawal of belligerents' forces to pre-war boundaries.

21 See Milan Hauner, *op. cit.*, p. 30.
22 See Lawrence Lifschultz, *op. cit.*, ''From the U-2 to the P-3...''
23 V. Ashitkov, K. Gevorkyan and V. Svetozarov, *The Truth About Afghanistan*. Novosti Press, Moscow, 1986, pp. 51-52.
24 Selig Harrison, ''The Shah, Not Kremlin, Touched Off Afghan Coup'', *Washington Post*, May 13, 1979.
25 Association of Southeast Asian Nations.

Indian Diplomacy*

ASHOK KAPUR**

ABSTRACT

Nehru was the symbol and the maker of Indian diplomacy after 1947 and the key spokesman on foreign affairs for the Indian Congress Party before 1947. His mental outlook and approach yielded a mixed legacy in foreign affairs. (1) His move towards the USSR produced *policy-development*. (2) His contradictory impulses *institutionalised ambivalence* in the Indian decision process concerning nuclear affairs, military policy and Pakistan policy. (3) His China policy produced *policy-failure*. Finally (4) his attitude towards India's smaller South Asian neighbours and Southeast Asian states produced *policy-neglect*. After Nehru, Indian diplomacy became power-oriented and interventionist; and the level of action shifted from the primacy of the global plane to that of regional and domestic planes. Indian diplomatic theory and practice in the Nehru and the post-Nehru eras reveal the presence of six competing approaches or sub-cultures. The debate between their assumptions and implications has not been settled in Indian thinking. Hence Indian diplomatic theory and practice are still evolving. Nehru's foreign affairs record deserves critical scrutiny in part to correct the mythology about his diplomacy and in part to get a true measure of his bitter-sweet legacy.

Critical Assessment of the Nehru Years

POST-1947 INDIAN DIPLOMATIC THEORY and practice were shaped exclusively up to 1964 by Prime Minister J. L. Nehru's mental outlook and egoism, his sense of Indian interests and his view of great power relations rather than by the requirements of any specific set of ideological and/or strategic principles. His mental outlook was vaguely Fabian. His mental or emotive reference points revealed (i) opposition to British racialism and colonialism, (ii) acceptance of the British model of parliamentary democracy and party system and (iii) sympathy for the Bolshevik revolution and the implied empathy between two subject nations.[1] The second element led Nehru to promote, in India, a Western-style party system where diverse and adversarial social and economic interests were meant to crystallise into a homogeneous political culture. But this conception of democracy is not Indian: individualism, diversity and a search for consensus among multiple points of view (which cannot be accommodated by a two- or a three-party system) is normal to Indians. In this respect Nehru's approach to Indian politics and political organisation was based on second-hand, un-Indian and alien concep-

* This paper draws on research supported by South Asia Ontario/Canadian Donner Foundation project.

** Department of Political Science, University of Waterloo, Waterloo, Canada.

tions. On the first point Nehru opposed British colonialism but his actions as Prime Minister revealed a contempt for South and Southeast Asians; they were patronising. Here again he was not original. On the third point, his embrace of Soviet socialism as a model for India's planned economy and socialist directive principles in India's Constitution revealed him to be a synthesiser[2] He was not a camp follower but he was not original. Egoism too played a key role in the foreign policy-making process. He created a one-man Foreign Office. From 1947 to 1964 he held the foreign affairs portfolio. The Cabinet's influence in foreign affairs was marginal at best because Nehru saw himself as the ultimate expert in all aspects of foreign affairs.[3] His speeches were rambling, not clearly logical and showed no sign of good staff work or drafting.

Nehru's grasp of military strategy was poor. His actions and military posture showed that he learnt nothing from ancient Indian diplomatic and military theories and practices. Nehru's writings and actions reveal a lack of understanding of the diplomatic and military practices of the East India Company and the British India Government, as they organised power relations with Indian princes, as they developed buffers on India's frontiers and as they managed land and seapower in relation to the Indian sub-continent. Nor did he learn much from world diplomatic and military history which could have been put to good use to advance Indian national interests as distinct from Nehru's. Hugh Tinker sees the makers of the newly independent states as dreamers, schemers or fighters. Nehru was neither a fighter nor a schemer but he was a dreamer. Non-alignment and peace diplomacy were his dreams, his pose. But as Nehru's successors learnt the hard way, non-alignment and world peace could not be substitutes for policy. These were an escape from the necessity to craft enduring power relations out of practical, immediate and long-range circumstances and imperatives.

The criticism is that Nehru was vague, ambivalent and unoriginal in his approach to Indian politics and foreign affairs and this negative effect on the orientation of India's political system has been enduring. He borrowed and synthesised foreign concepts and applied them to Indian conditions. His success was the result of favorable domestic and external circumstances viz., the love and trust which the Indian people bestowed on the Nehrus; the absence of a political alternative to rule by the Nehrus; and the willingness of foreign powers to help Indian development and security. Nehru-ism flourished under these circumstances. But beneath the aura of success is a picture of short term gain and long term problems which are of a structural nature. Nehru style parliamentary democracy which was Nehru-centric and Congress Party-centric distorted India's political development because it created a form of guided democracy which was managed from the top, the Centre. Furthermore, the development of India's foreign policy mechanism was retarded. Foreign policy is ultimately made by non-expert political leaders in most countries. For this reason political leaders choose their expert advisers carefully. Under Nehru, Indian foreign policy was a one-man, Nehru-centric policy.

This approach lasted from 1947 to 1964. It damaged the foundation of Indian foreign policy thinking.

Yet, despite vagueness in style and ambivalence in content, and despite known failures of salient aspects of Nehru's policies especially on China, military affairs and South Asian regionalism, Nehru-ism has not been disowned; indeed it continues to be praised[4] Western powers continue to like Nehru because he made India into a bastion of West-oriented neo-colonialism[5] in the third world, then and now a critical long term arena of the East-West struggle for diplomatic influence, military bases and economic interests. The Soviet bloc including Eastern Europe continues to praise the Nehru non-alignment because the India connection has helped Soviet diplomatic and military interests in the Third World against American and Chinese competition. Only China (Chou-en-Lai in the 1960s) and successive Pakistani leaders denounced Nehru. All Pakistani governments have also denounced Hindus and Indians as well. Being India's enemies, Pakistani and Chinese critique carry no credibility with Indian public opinion. Nehru's followers in the Congress Party and in the Indian Foreign Office had their own reasons not to criticise Nehru. They admired him for standing up to the great powers. They benefitted from his patronage and they were content to be yes-men and to work within the Nehru-type political-administrative system. Finally, they saw no alternative to a Nehru-istic India since neither a Gandhian India nor a Patel-type rightist India nor a RSS-type communal India nor a J. P. Narayan-type India appealed to the Congress Party and the Indian administrative elites.

The suggestion here is that the content of India's foreign policy since the Nehru days reflects India's weak internal and economic situation, its neo-colonial political culture (exploitation, manipulation and bargaining among horizontal and vertical cleavages in India) and its neo-colonial situation in the post-1945 world power structure. In this perspective, according to Nehru's critics, India's main enemy is within, i.e., in the orientation of India's political system as shaped by the Nehrus and their followers. In this perspective, the so called successes of the Nehru type of non-aligned "policy" planted seeds of long term structural problems for Indians and Nehru's political successors. Hence short term successes must be judged to be long term failures of Indian diplomacy. The critics' contention is that India's political/foreign policy system has placed India in a neo-colonial situation in economic and diplomatic affairs in the post-1945 world. This "system" requires continuous manipulation of Indian political and economic processes from the top. It further requires continuous rejection of alternatives to the Nehru approach to economic, political and diplomatic affairs. This system works. It holds India together. But it is not truly democratic in domestic affairs because it has failed to achieve nation-building on the basis of consensus-development out of diverse Indian social, political, economic, religious interests and points of view. Such diversity cannot be managed by the straight jacket of a single political party or even a multi-party parliamentary system, or a noisy, inexpert Parliament. In economic affairs Nehru failed to move the country towards policies which would make a big difference to the plight of the poor. In external relations Nehru failed both to gain military security on India's borders and to enhance India's reputation in either the inner councils of the great powers or among India's neighbours in the sub-continent. The charge against Nehru is that he managed India's domestic and to some extent its foreign affairs but that he did not transform India into a strong consensus-oriented modern society or policy. Rather he managed to develop Indian political institutions with a new face (viz., Congress Party, all-India services, planning commission) but this was done on old lines. If anything he transformed India into a neo-colonial India after the retreat of British power from India; that is, Nehru embraced the substance but not the style of the British colonial model of administrative management because that suited his mental outlook and life experiences.

To make sense of Nehru's legacy to Indian politics and Indian political and military diplomacy it is necessary to evaluate his foreign affairs record according to several analytical cuts. The Nehru years as prime minister and foreign minister were overshadowed by the image of India's and Nehru's defeat at China's hands in 1962. In fact, Nehru's legacy is broader and more complex than the 1962 image indicates. His foreign affairs record contains elements of policy success, policy failure, ambivalent policy, distorted development, conceptual innovation and conceptual error. To measure each element it is necessary to consider the record in terms of its results during and after Nehru's lifetime.

The following cuts help us specify Nehru's negative and positive contributions as well as the grey areas.

A. Where Nehru's diplomacy (assessment and policy) failed him and India during his lifetime

This refers specifically to his China policy. Nehru's thinking about the nature of Sino-Soviet relations was correct. In the early 1950s he correctly estimated the existence of cracks in the Sino-Soviet front and the need for the West and India to exploit it.[6] But he misjudged the implication of this factor for Indian diplomacy and Indian security. His policy of building bridges vis-a-vis China, trusting China and not confronting it were flawed. His China policy was cast in the framework of his conception of Asian unity with China and India as it main pillars. His China policy also meant a pre-occupation with the great powers and a neglect of South Asian and Southeast Asian small states who were India's neighbours and its economic, cultural and diplomatic frontiers. Here Nehru's lack of preparation against China and with the small Asian states set back Indian security on its northern front and injured India's diplomatic, cultural and economic influence in the small states in South and Southeast Asia. Overall, it produced neither short term nor long term gains for Indian interests.

B. Where Nehru's contradictory impulses produced ambivalent policies

Brecher[7] emphasises Nehru's indecisiveness in decision-making. Eric Stokes, however, correctly points to Nehru's contradictory impulses.[8] Ambivalence should not be equated with failure but ambivalence in India's nuclear policy, its military policy and its Pakistan policy created a framework of foreign policy action with built-in contradictions, oscillations and paralysis. This encouraged domestic controversies and oscillatory pressures in the decision process in these areas. Nehru's speeches on Indian nuclear affairs during 1946-48 revealed four components: the importance of secrecy; his preference for peaceful use of atomic energy; its potential for "other purposes" if India is "compelled"; and the need to stay abreast of modern developments. His military policy oscillated between using limited military force to manage external aggression (Kashmir; Goa) and on the other hand, leaving power vacuums on India's China border which invited Chinese military pressure. His Pakistan policy oscillated between a search for friendship with Pakistan and the opposition to Pakistan-US-China ties. The argument here is that by failing to provide central direction, and by creating instead an ambivalent base of policy action, Nehru created opportunities for development of domestic—intra-governmental and intra-societal—controversies. These distorted the steady development of policies in areas which were critical to India's strategic well-being. Furthermore, the presence of build-in domestic vetoes sapped internal political will, it created organisational disunity and it retarded policy development. Nehru's ambivalence in these areas reflected two contradictory impulses, viz., utopianism and globalism on the one hand, and realism and a concern with Indian interests on the other hand. Here his mental outlook and ambivalent policy actions had enduring effects and left behind a bitter legacy in the form of unsettled debates about India's nuclear and Pakistan policies.

C. Where Nehru made positive contributions to Indian diplomatic thinking and to Indian diplomatic policy by laying the foundation of a geo-political strategy

My contention is that the geo-political side of Nehru's diplomacy is revealed not by his military and nuclear activities (which were neglected) but by his diplomatic actions towards the USSR during 1950-53. The contention is that Nehru contributed to policy development by building a diplomatic bridge to Moscow. This enabled him and his successors to connect Indian diplomacy to the superpowers' diplomacy with results that benefitted Indian interests.

A concern to shape diplomatic alignments with the great powers of the time, i.e., a concern with practical power politics rather than ideological considerations, determined Nehru's quest for the Moscow connection. According to the literature in 1954 the US-Pakistan military supply relationship emerged, and by 1955 a meeting of minds occurred between Pakistani and Chinese leaders.[9] With the crystallisation of adverse foreign alignments against Indian interests in the mid-1950s, regional pressures induced India to turn to the USSR as an external partner. This view of history is correct but it is incomplete. My contention is that concern with power relations guided Nehru's USSR diplomacy from 1950 itself. In the 1950-53 period the arena of this diplomacy was the world stage. At the time there were no major internal and external pressures on India to turn towards Moscow. Favourable external circumstances, Nehru's egotistical desire to be a world statesman and his quest to put India on the world map, rather than pressing domestic or regional compulsions, governed his quest for the Moscow connection.

Nehru's move to establish strong Indo-Soviet links and to achieve a meeting of minds with Stalin was innovative. It reflected a play with the psychological plane of diplomacy where the organisation of inter-state relations is effected by addressing the mental outlook of the political leader on the other side. In his approach to Stalin (1950-53) Nehru was neither indecisive (Brecher's characterisation of Nehru), nor was his policy the result of contradictory impulses (Erik Stokes' characterisation of Nehru). Rather, overlapping motives converged to lead to a Delhi-Moscow connection. Nehru's motives were partly egotistical (to create a name for Nehru); partly ideological (Nehru's leftist orientation); partly a concern to protect Indian national interests in the international arena by effecting Indian access to all the major power centres, by having opportunities to moderate their actions in world affairs; and partly to seek their support for Indian strategic interests. The timing of Nehru's secret overtures to Stalin was before the US-Pakistan alignment crystallised in 1953-54. The tilt in Nehru's mind and in Indian diplomacy towards the USSR occurred by Indian choice, as a result of Nehru's initiative and not as a result of domestic and external compulsions. By sketching the timing and the nature of Nehru's move towards Stalin we find that Nehru changed the framework of Soviet diplomatic thinking by revealing to it the opportunities and obligations for the USSR in India and in the Third World. Furthermore, by his tilt towards Moscow in the 1950-53 period Nehru laid the foundation of the Indo-Soviet link which acquired enduring value for both sides.

The Nehru initiative towards Stalin is comparable to the Jinnah initiative towards the US government (1947-48).[10] The parallels are that the USA responded to Jinnah's initiative after his death and Stalin responded to Nehru's in his lifetime. The sequence of initiatives and results was somewhat as follows. Jinnah made his overture to the US government in August, 1947 claiming that Pakistan's main fears centered on Russian expansionism and Hindu imperialism. The US government was not initially responsive. Then came the disastrous Nehru visit to the USA. This was followed by Nehru's initiative towards Stalin, which was well known to Western embassies in Moscow. Then came the shift in the US position, from neutrality in Indo-Pakistan affairs to a tilt towards Pakistan. Finally, by the mid-1950s Moscow's tilty towards India became clear by its support of India's Kashmir policy. The Jinnah-US, and the Nehru-Stalin moves indicate an important truth: great powers do not always seek opportunities to co-opt lesser powers into their activities but lesser powers often develop opportunities to co-opt the great powers into their plans.

Nehru's leftist outlook conditioned him to look favourably on Moscow and his mistrust of Western power politics conditioned him to look unfavourably on America's containment policy and its reliance on military pressures to settle political disputes. But this outlook should not be seen as an ideological drive to join the Soviet camp because Nehru's "socialism" reflected contradictory impulses whereas his USSR policy did not. Nehru's socialism was a potpourri: concern with social and economic issues—yes; class war—no; collectivism—yes; individualism—yes; coercion under certain conditions—yes, but generally—no; compromise and conciliation was the preferred method of political action for Nehru but coercion under certain conditions was also acceptable.[11] Nehru's socialism was not the determinant of the Nehru-Stalin linkup; Nehru's egoism was a major determinant but not the sole one. Practical considerations affected Nehru's move towards Stalin. In part Nehru mistrusted the Indian Left and its quest for an Indian revolution.[12] Here domestic compulsions—the quest to ensure the Congress Party's and Nehru's dominance of the Indian political system and the subordination of the Indian Left—was a motive for foreign policy action, among other motives mentioned earlier. Here Nehru was seeking a triangular relationship between Moscow, Nehru's India and the Indian Left. Here the primacy of foreign policy considerations was likely to induce Moscow to use its influence to moderate the revolutionary impulses of the Indian Left and to ensure the dominance of the Nehru-led Congress Party in Indian politics. To an assessment of the setting of Indo-Soviet affairs and the line of Nehru's approach to Stalin and its consequence for Indian diplomacy we now turn.

Nehru's move towards Stalin occurred in the 1949-50 period in the context of Nehru's disastrous visit to the USA in 1949. At this time there was no pressing security problem on India's borders except for Pakistani military pressure in Kashmir which was manageable. India-China relations were friendly. Within India Nehru was popular. But Delhi-Moscow relations were icy. During the Second World War Indian troops had been moved around in different military theatres under British command and Stalin saw them as mercenaries, not freedom fighters, and India as a British colony. The year 1947 made little impact on Stalin's thinking. He saw it as an imperial game and Lord Louis Mountbatten, Viceroy turned Indian Governor General as the reigning imperial deity in India. Moreover, the partition left the impression that Indian and Pakistani independence might be short-lived. In Stalin's eyes India in 1947 was still a creature of imperialist powers. During 1947-49 Madame Vijalakshmi Pandit, Nehru's sister, was India's ambassador to the USSR. Stalin ignored her presence, refused to receive her, and treated her with contempt by literally confining her to Indian embassy walls. Pandit was aristocratic and arrogant, and Stalin's ill-treatment affected her psychological condition in Moscow. This was reported to Stalin but he did not relent towards

Nehru's sister. The official mood and attitude towards India was revealed by the Soviet press which dubbed India as "imperialist lackeys, running dogs".

This was the background in which Dr. S. Radhakrishnan was sent to Moscow to replace Madame Pandit. The choice was calculated. Nehru was being typically Nehru when he sent his sister, a symbol of affluence, to a Russia which was recovering from the ravages of the war. Dr. S. Radhakrishnan was a philosopher and philosophers were respected in the USSR and China, who were then great friends. Nehru thought that Radhakrishnan might fit into the Moscow scene. Stalin however didn't much care. A deputy foreign minister received his credentials, a sign of low standing in the host country's estimation. The tirades in the Soviet press against Nehru continued but these were not accurately reported to the Indian prime minister by the Indian embassy in Moscow.

In these circumstances two developments occurred which established the foundation of Indo-Soviet ties. The first, initiated by Radhakrishnan was to cultivate persons in the confidence of Stalin and to give the impression that the declaration of India as a republic (1950 constitution) was done at the instance of Radhakrishnan who in turn was greatly inspired by the Soviet Republic and the fortitude of its great leader, Stalin—the man of iron. Side by side came the propaganda that philosopher Radhakrishnan slept for only two hours and worked on his philosophical works all night, and Stalin was missing a man of great profundity who equally admired a profound world leader like Stalin. The approach that Stalin was missing something in not meeting Radhakrishnan worked. In 1950 Radhakrishnan became known in Soviet circles as the philosopher who did not sleep. Being heavy drinkers and sleepers this mystified Russians. (The Radhakrishnan line, however, had no impact on Western diplomats in Moscow.)

This softening of Soviet hostility to Nehru and India coincided with the second development which concerned the Korean war. Indian diplomacy in Korea went through at least two main volte-faces. The first one led to Indian support for the US resolution at the UN which led to the creation of South Korea and the partition of the two Koreas.[13] This was seen as a pro-US act by the parties concerned. The second one, which had a positive effect in changing Stalin's view of Nehru's India, occured after the Chinese unleashed their military forces against General MacArthur's armies. The Chinese military tactics required the use of massive manpower. This was a new approach for Western armies which depended on the importance of conserving manpower in war. China's sweeping advance against MacArthur's forces put the USA in a dilemma. They needed a ceasefire immediately in the peninsula through the UN and they canvassed the UN-members for a ceasefire at the 38th parallel. Nehru and many non-communist states agreed and this created jubilation in the non-communist camp and gloom among the communists. At this point the Soviet government pressured Nehru, through its Delhi channels, to change its position, not to vote for the US resolution, and to prove by deeds the Radhakrishnan effort to ingratiate Nehru with Stalin. The pressure was successful. Nehru reversed his position on the 38th parallel ceasefire and this volte-face revealed to Stalin the opportunity to encourage a parting of the ways between Delhi and Washington and to bring India to the Soviet side in Korean affairs. This specific deed was a turning point in Indo-Soviet and Indo-US relations. It reinforced the Radhakrishnan line to Moscow that he had influence over Nehru and that he had a plan to settle the Korea issue which required Radhakrishnan-Stalin consultations. This led Stalin to give an interview to Radhakrishnan, a rare event in Moscow at the time. At this crucial meeting, Radhakrishnan impressed Stalin with Nehru's socialist leanings and his attitude to the Spanish war, among other stands. Here for the first time India, through its ambassador in Moscow, articulated the notion that Soviet Russia was truly a pre-dominantly Asian power, and that it was in her interests to encourage the East in foreign affairs; and India in the East could be a strong influence if it were encouraged and cultivated by Moscow. Stalin agreed to encourage India provided India showed its good faith by deeds. The Nehru volte-face on the 38th parallel issue was the gift which sealed the Nehru-Stalin bargain.

During the Nehru years, Nehru's mental outlook, and external opportunities and circumstances (rather than severe pressures), and to a lesser degree, domestic circumstances shaped his diplomatic activities. Nehru was an autonomous player in the Indian political system and in the international system. India on the whole was not constrained by domestic and external pressures. Still only a few of his assessments were sound. (1) He correctly anticipated the Sino-Soviet conflict and the need to expoit the differences to Indian advantage. Here the theory was not to stay aloof from external power relations but to play both sides to his (Nehru's) and India's advantage. Here the theory was not to seek reduction of tension between the two communist states but rather to build on the tensions. (2) Nehru also correctly used this approach in his policy of "equi-adjacence"[14] bilateralism towards the two superpowers from 1949 onwards. (3) Where Nehru went wrong was that he assumed that Indian security was protected by the global balance of power; that the superpowers had a common interest in curbing China's ambitions; that economic and social development (peaceful activity) alone was sufficient for Indian defence; and that India could achieve international status by peace diplomacy and East-West bridge building alone. A corollary mistake of fundamental proportions was that even after external alignments began to crystallise against Indian interests from the mid-1950s onwards through the development of Sino-Pakistani-American relations, Nehru remained wedded to his old ideas. He was original in his assessments of great power relations in the post-war period but he was not original in responding to external pressures against India. For almost a decade (1955-1964) Nehru lived in his own dream world and left India internally and externally weak. In regional security issues Nehru was neither practical nor insightful. He failed to see that Indian status in world affairs required development of internal economic, political *and military* strength; that world status could come about temporarily by other means, i.e., if external circumstances such as the Cold War in the late 1940s favoured third party bridge builders like India, but that once these particular circumstances changed, the status could change as easily. (Nehru was of no direct use to the superpowers after the Korean war and after the superpowers learnt to talk directly.)

Under these circumstances, the main turning point in the development of Indian diplomatic theory and practice during the Nehru years was in the 1949-50 period when Nehru and Ambassador Radhakrishnan achieved a breakthrough with Stalin. This process laid the foundation of Nehru's equi-adjacense policy vis-a-vis the superpowers. Its impact was far-reaching. From that time on, all Indian governments have remained tilted towards Moscow. As signs of this tilt, note Nehru's ambivalence about Soviet military action against Hungary, the volte-face on the 38th parallel issue, Indian support of Soviet disarmament positions at the UN, and Indian legitimisation of Soviet activities in the third world where Indo-Soviet relations serve as a model, and the USSR is projected as a natural ally of non-alignment. This tilt however, should not be seen as Indian dependence as is usually done by American scholars and pamphleteers. Nehru's USSR policy was in the context of his basic concept of "equi-adjacence" and his rejection of "equi-distance". Here Nehru contributed to both theory-development and Indian policy-development. This commitment to the concept of equi-adjacence has never been lost by Indian diplomatic practitioners. This may be viewed as the common ground in Indian public and diplomatic opinion during the last 40 years. It also meant that in Nehru's theory and practice, but not in his public relations or posture, Indian non-alignment was really bi-alignment with both bloc leaders; that is, Nehru embraced the notion of bipolarity and the international status quo as the basis of Indian policy. Here again Nehru was clever but not original in his thinking.

The Orientation of Indian Diplomacy After Nehru

'What does independence consist of? It consists fundamentally and basically of foreign relations. That is the test of independence. All else is local autonomy.[15] This was Nehru's definition, and "foreign relations" to him meant the advancement of Indian interests, India's status in world affairs, India's peaceful internal development and its external security. On these tests, i.e., on Nehru's own terms, his legacy to India, to his dynasty, was bittersweet. The positive side was that his successors inherited and embraced and developed his concept of equi-adjacence and bi-alignment with the superpowers. But the bitter legacy was revealed in the tasks which Nehru's successors had to undertake as a result of his mistakes. These tasks were: (1) to consolidate Indian political and military authority in border areas within the Indian Union; (2) to manage external military pressures on Indian borders; and (3) to escape the coercive effects of hostile external diplomatic and military alignments which threatened India's territorial integrity and which created domestic controversies about economic, military and diplomatic policies. These tasks emerged because Nehru had neglected South Asian regionalism; he neglected to develop Indian military power; and he neglected to publicise and to prepare against the hostile external coalitions as they were taking shape. He should have been attending to regional geo-politics instead of dancing on the world stage; he should have attended to problems of Indian security and regional power instead of the world's problems.

Elsewhere I have outlined the compulsions which governed the diplomatic and military actions of Nehru's successors.[16] Broadly, Indian actions in the 1965 and 1971 wars were turning points in sub-continental military affairs. The 1965 war revealed the Shastri concept that if Pakistan put military pressure on Kashmir, then India would put military pressure on Pakistan itself and create an internal controversy within Pakistan and in the military regime as well. The 1971 war revealed another concept: that India was no longer committed to the territorial status quo. It was no longer committed to the military doctrine of territorial defence but that it was willing to engage in military intervention (but not conquest) to break up a modern state (Pakistan) and to create a new one (Bangladesh). Both events created new precedents in post-1945, post-colonial international relations. This war was a turning point in another way. It revealed a willingness to use military force to damage the two-nation theory (the psychological foundation of Pakistan) by encouraging and facilitating, the revolt of Bangladeshi nationalism (or sub-nationalism). India's 1971 action highlights an enduring problem, and the opportunities for India, of competitive sub-nationalisms and regional pressures in Pakistan's political system since 1947. In these two major instances, India military force was employed to manage inter-state military relations as well as to direct events and to move sub-national and regional socio-political tendencies in neighbouring states towards particular results.

Despite this remarkable evolution of Indian military strategy, Indian diplomatic strategy in the post-Nehru eras continued to oscilliate between six sets of assumptions, policy implications and sub-cultures in the Indian political system.

1) The oldest, Nehru's favourite, which was repudiated by the 1962 India-China war, but which has continuing popular appeal especially among the Gandians and Western and Soviet supporters of Indian utopianism, was that India's real front in world affairs was internal. That strength lay in internal economic, social and political development by peaceful means. This simply meant a parliamentary democracy, a mixed but planned economy, socialist slogans and a commitment to peaceful change. The idea was that India should not allow external differences to intrude into the theory and practice of her peaceful development. The implication was that India should settle differences with hostile foreign powers by peaceful means; hence the fascination with peaceful co-existence, world peace, global humanism and One World concepts.

2) After the Sino-Pakistan diplomatic and military relationship crystallised, the view emerged that China and Pakistan are but a single enemy; that it was not possible to differentiate between the two; and that it was necessary to prepare to fight both at the military and psychological levels of action. This view and approach to diplomacy and military affairs was prominent in Indian elite and popular thinking especially during the 1960s. This view, however, is not wholly valid. The crisis behaviour of Pakistan and China reveals the presence of restraint on the principle that one should not take advantage of the enemy's temporary difficulties. Thus, Pakistan did not attack India in 1962. And China did not attack India in the 1965 and 1971 wars. Still, this dual concern persists as the worst military contingency analysis and because of the public identification of Pakistan and China as India's main external enemies.

3) After the emergence of the India-China problem, the view emerged that India cannot fight its diplomatic and military battles on both the China and the Pakistan fronts. Hence, given the danger to India from China, India (according to this view) ought to settle with Pakistan, a smaller neighbour, because the two countries belong to the Indian sub-continent, and both have a common outlook concerning sub-continental security and both have common internal problems regarding nation-building. This is the approach of the pro-Pakistan lobby in India. This view has endured since 1947 and it was reinforced by the India-China border war.

4) This view shares the premise of the third one, viz., that India cannot fight on both the China and the Pakistan fronts. But the fourth view regards the Pakistan threat as the greater danger to Indian security than the China threat. Here the premise is that Pakistan is India's natural and permanent enemy; China is less so and not inevitably so; and there is no natural or historical enmity between the Indian and the Chinese peoples and the two countries. The implication is that once an India-China border settlement is achieved then India can face Pakistan with full military might and thus settle the Pakistan problem by force. Elements of this approach are revealed in the Rajiv Gandhi government's on-going negotiations with China and his hard line against Pakistan's military modernisation and nuclear weapons programme.

5) The premise here is that India can comfortably manage to contain both the Pakistan and China military and diplomatic fronts, and indeed it has, since 1971, managed the pressures against India's interests by the superpowers as well. That is, there is no need for India to make concessions to foreign powers to relieve their pressure against Indian interests. The implication of this approach is that continuing Indian military modernisation is necessary to ensure the continued utility of this approach. Another implication is that the main task of Indian diplomacy is not to settle bilateral problems and to organise Indian concessions but rather it is to ensure the flow of timely and accurate diplomatic intelligence to the India decisionmakers. Another implication is that even though there is no urgency to settle pending diplomatic issues

with hostile powers and with India's neighbours, the task of diplomacy is to keep the lines of communication open with the parties concerned, i.e., keep talking without necessarily trying hard to achieve agreement through concessions. Elements of this apprach are also revealed in the approach of the Indian governments since 1971.

6) Here the task of Indian diplomacy and military policy is not simply to protect Indian borders. It is also to guard Indian frontiers, i.e., to prevent the emergence of hostile foreign coalitions in the frontier zones beyond its territorial boundaries. The development of the Indian defence forces' interventionist capabilities and Indian diplomatic and military actions in Sri Lanka (1983-) and its diplomacy in Afghanistan (1985-) point to the presence of this sub-culture. (In Sri Lanka, India's objective was to prevent the emergence of a hostile Sri-Lanka-Pakistan-USA-Israel coalition. In Afghanistan it is to secure a non-aligned Afghanistan and to avoid the rise of a pro-Pakistan fundamentalist Afghanistan).

At different points in India's diplomatic history one or the other or select combinations of these approaches have had an edge in the Indian decision-making process. Which approach predominates at a particular time has depended in a big way on the personal inclination of the Prime Minister. A sign of the ambivalence in Nehru's diplomatic thinking is that his stated views and actions in diplomatic affairs revealed a preference for the first approach and neglect of the others; and yet these approaches emerged as a consequence of the inadequacies of the first one. By failing to examine the other approaches in terms of Indian policy requirements, Nehru's overall record was not one of directing events or providing specific policy direction in the foreign affairs field. By weakening India's internal and external security position, he broadened the scope of internal controversy and ambivalence in the framework of Indian diplomatic thinking as revealed by the existence of competing approaches. Furthermore, by making the Indian Foreign Office into a Nehru-dominated institution, the Nehrus neutralised independent centres of policy advice within the bureaucracy. Had they existed, they could have settled the ever-present debate between the six approaches in Indian diplomatic theory and practice. To this day the Indian Foreign Office has failed to acquire the institutional strength and the intellectual prowess to settle on a choice between the six approaches and to publicise the guiding principles of Indian diplomatic strategy. This reveals a paralysis of "thought power". It is a pity that by creating a Nehru-dominated Foreign Office Nehru and his successors retarded innovative Indian diplomatic thinking within the Foreign Office even though the Indian foreign service is well-trained and among the best in the world in terms of its ability to execute a brief. This problem is even more acute among Indian scholars who rarely function outside the framework of the six official approaches. Instead, Nehru preserved for himself and his successors a tradition of Nehru-centric, ad hoc, and personality-oriented rather than theme-centric or issue-centric diplomacy which could influence international thinking and events. This is why Indian military action had been most effective when the mandate is clear, i.e., to defend Indian borders; and it is less so when the official mandate, as in the case of the Golden Temple and Sri Lankan actions, is muddled by ambivalence in the diplomatic machinery concerning the nature of the front and the desirable line of diplomatic and military action. Nehru is dead but his legacy of ambivalence in Indian diplomatic strategy continues to haunt the corridors of the Indian Foreign Office.

NOTES

1 Hugh Tinker, *Men Who Overturned Empires, Fighters, Dreamers and Schemers*, Macmillan Press, London, 1987, Ch. 4.
2 T. A. Keenleyside, "Origins of Indian Foreign Policy: A Study of Indian Nationalist Attitudes to Foreign Affairs, 1927-39," unpublished Ph.D. Thesis, University of London, 1966.
3 S. Gopal, *Jawaharlal Nehru, A Biography*, Harvard University Press, Cambridge, Mass., vol. 2, 1947-1956, 1979, p. 54, note 49. K.P.S. Menon, *Many Worlds*, Oxford University Press, London, 1965, p. 271 maintains that India's "foreign policy therefore necessarily rested on the intuition of one man, who was Foreign Minister as well as Prime Minister, Jawaharlal Nehru."
4 This is especially true of Indian scholarship, especially "committed" Indian scholarship. See for instance, S. Gopal, *ibid.* G. Parathasarthi, ed., *Jawaharlal Nehru: Letters to Chief Ministers, 1947-64*, vol. 1, 1947-49, Oxford University Press, Delhi, 1985.
5 The suggestion is that most Western powers objected to particular Nehru policies, e.g. Hungary (1956), but overall they considered him as one of their own men. Several Western comments make this clear. In the early years (1947-49), Nehru was transparently pro-West and suspicious of the USSR. These attitudes became opaque in subsequent years. "Neo-colonialism" implies integration of a weaker economy with that of the stronger powers; accomodation of interests of elites in the "centre" and the "periphery"; and marginalisation of the poor in the "periphery". These signs were present in the relationships between Nehru's India and the superpowers and lesser Western powers. Nehru was overtly nationalistic and non-aligned and glorified "Indianness" but these images do not rescue him from the charge that he induced India's dependence on foreign powers in economic and political affairs; and that "nationalism is imperialism by other means". Instead of developing Indian solutions for Indian problems he sought foreign solutions and concepts in political, economic and military affairs. In Marxist analysis, "neo-colonialism" reflects the premise of economic determinism. My usage of the term is broader and concerns India's economic, political and military relations with the economic and military powers of the time in the Nehru era.
6 Escott Reid, *Envoy to Nehru*, Oxford University Press, Toronto, 1981, pages 247-48, 12, 57.
7 M. Brecher, *Nehru, A Political Biography*, Oxford University Press, London, 1959, p. 627.
8 E. Stokes, "Jawaharlal Nehru in the Making," (Review), *Modern Asian Studies*, II, 2 (1977), p. 295.
9 Sisir Gupta, *Kashmir, A Study in India-Pakistan Relations*, Asia Publishing House, 1966, pp. 423-24.
10 M. S. Venkataramani, *The American Role in Pakistan, 1947-58*, Radiant Publishers, 1982, Chapters 1-4.
11 Furthermore, in Nehru's outlook. US foreign policy was "naive", "immature", and "lacking in intelligence". See S. Gopal, *op. cit.*, pages 44, 59, 60, and 63. On Nehru's socialism see M. N. Das, *The Political Philosophy of Jawaharlal Nehru*, Georg Allen & Unwin, London, 1961, Chapter 5.
12 Nehru's concern about the Indian Left and its Soviet ties is revealed in his confidential memoranda (1950). See Gopal, *op. cit.* pages 44 and 64.

13 K. P. S. Menon, *op. cit.* p. 257.

14 Up to 1949 Nehru seemed to follow a policy of "equi-distance" towards the USA and the USSR. See Nehru's note of January 1947 to his officials as reported in K. P. S. Menon, *ibid.*, p. 229; and S. Gopal, *op. cit.* p. 44. The concept of "equi-adjacence" is from Sisir Gupta, in M. S. Rajan and S. Ganguly, eds. *Sisir Gupta: India and the International System*, Vikas Publishing House, New Delhi, 1981, p. 25. Nehru's shift in 1949-50 from "equi-distance" to "equi-adjacence", therefore, concerned policy as well as thought.

15 Nehru, speech in the Constituent Assembly, 8 March, 1949, as quoted in S. Gopal, *op. cit.* p. 300.

16 A. Kapur, "Indian Security and Defence Policies Under Indira Gandhi," *Journal of Asian and African Studies*, vol. XXII, nos. 3-4, July and Oct. 1987, pp. 175-193.

The Foreign Policies of India's Immediate Neighbours A Reflective Interpretation

A. JEYARATNAM WILSON*

ABSTRACT

The foreign policies of Nepal, Bhutan, Bangladesh and Sri Lanka have focussed mainly on Indian security concerns. These states have avoided a clash with India. Where clashes occurred, as in India-Nepal relations, 1950 and India-Sri Lanka relations, 1987, India intervened to stress her claims. India's relationship with Pakistan has been unsatisfactory. Both states feed on each other's military insecurity. In 1948 Sri Lanka had similar fears. However, its participation in the nonalignment movement has been in harmony with India's. Pakistan sought admission and joined the US alliance network against the USSR. Pakistan's trajectory invites US and PRC interest and India has secured a position with the Indo-Soviet Treaty, 1971. The involvement by major power threatens South Asian peace. The SAARC is neither a solution for economic nor for political problems. South Asia should be recognised as a sub-system for international purposes. In that event the meddling of foreign powers in a volatile area can be monitored by the United Nations to restore confidence and stability in the region.

THE FOREIGN POLICIES of one group of states, the Himalayan (Nepal, Bhutan and Sikkim), and Bangladesh and Sri Lanka are affected by India, the dominant power in the region. The rule was well laid down by India's first Prime Minister, Jawaharlal Nehru, on 6 January, 1950 in a statement to the Indian Parliament on Nepal (a policy pronouncement which has been applied to all the states in this group):[1]

> ... much as we appreciate the independence of Nepal, we cannot allow anything to go wrong in Nepal or permit that barrier to be crossed or weakened, because that would be a risk to our own security

Nepal was in "the throes of a revolution that threatened to result in political chaos."[2] Indian policy towards Sikkim, Bhutan, East Pakistan (Bangladesh since 1971) and Sri Lanka (since the Indo-Sri Lanka Peace Accord of 29 July, 1987) was based on the same consideration as were applied by Nehru to Nepal.

The second group of states is in a category of one, the Republic of Pakistan. Pakistan has resented India's intervention in Kashmir since April 1951 as well as Indian intervention in 1971 in East Pakistan which resulted in the emergence of the Republic of Bangladesh. Pakistan's foreign policies are,

* Department of Political Science, University of New Brunswick, Fredericton, Canada.

therefore, based on a fear of India on the one hand and a desire to challenge India's status as the major regional power on the other.

The concept of "Finlandization" could apply to the first group. By this we mean that the states in this group are obliged or compelled to adopt foreign policies which are not in conflict with the security interests of India; just as Finland cannot, in its external relations, threaten the national security of the USSR. Nehru's policy was re-stated by Mrs. Indira Gandhi in more emphatic terms, in the view of this writer, because of greater challenges to India's geostrategy in the region. In July 1983, Bharat Wariavwalla wrote in *The Round Table* what he termed the *national security state* of "Indira's (Gandhi) India".[3] He meant that India under Mrs. Gandhi was characterised by high defence spending, mobilisation of the country's strengths against an external enemy ("often imaginary"), the creation of a sense of beleagueredness and "an expansionist foreign policy". (The last-mentioned, in our view, was due to threats to India's security). Mrs. Gandhi in fact was strengthening India's position in a more difficult context along the lines of her father's (Nehru) Nepal policy laid down in January, 1950. Mrs. Gandhi's successor, Rajiv Gandhi therefore acted no differently when political chaos and internal rebellion threatened the disintegration of Sri Lanka.

To take the first group of states. Their foreign policies have either been "Finlandized" to various degrees or, alternatively, they have permitted some leeway so long as India's interests were not placed in jeopardy. Sikkim and Bhutan came into India's sphere of influence because of Indian uncertainties regarding the People's Republic of China (PRC). Nepal, Sri Lanka (until 1987) and Bangladesh were either manipulated or permitted freedom within a given safety network. (We consider the period 1947 to present times in respect of these states).

In case of Sikkim, that country was faced with internal destabilisation and consequently became a problem to India's security. Indian intervention, therefore, followed the familiar lines. In June 1949, the Chogyal or King of Sikkim, invited India to help with its internal disturbances. And on 5 December, 1950, India signed a Treaty of Perpetuity with Sikkim which made Sikkim an Indian protectorate. Between 1962-73, India made known its disapproval of the new Chogyal who had ascended the throne in 1963.[4] But it was not until 1973 with Mrs. Indira Gandhi as Prime Minister that India intervened. The immediate pretext was disaffection among Sikkim's Nepali-speaking majority. The Chogyal appealed to India for help. An agreement pledged that India would maintain law and order as well as Sikkim's internal administration. Internal reforms by way of an elected legislature with the Chogyal as formal head of state were instituted. In 1974, the elected legislature resolved that Sikkim should be annexed by India. In February 1975, Sikkim became part of the Indian union. These moves were to ensure India's security. India's moves in Sikkim in the period 1973-4 were guided by K. S. Bajpai, a top-ranking political officer. India has utilised the best possible skills in its diplomatic service in dealings with regional states.[5]

India was as successful in securing dominance over Bhutan. Bhutan was a sensitive area as was Sikkim, because of its proximity to the PRC. In August 1949, India signed a Treaty of Perpetual Peace and Friendship with Bhutan. India guaranteed non-interference in the internal affairs of Bhutan. Bhutan agreed to be guided by India's advice in external relations. In 1959, with Sino-Indian relations reaching a low ebb, Nehru urged Bhutan to agree to establishing a road link with India. Indian troops, it was agreed, would go to Bhutan's assistance in the event of an emergency. On 28 August, 1959, Nehru in a statement to the Lok Sabha, guaranteed the territorial integrity and the borders of Bhutan (and Sikkim). He added that aggression against either of these countries would be considered as aggression against India.[6] The obvious reference was to the PRC.

In the decade of the nineteen sixties, Bhutan had the twin problem of protesting the PRC's incorporation of a neighbouring Llamaist region, Tibet (Bhutan had the same Llamaist Buddhistic traditions), and of keeping India's presence in Bhutan at a low profile because of opposition from sections of the Bhutanese Buddhist elites to India's interference with their country and India's substantial presence there.

Again India's problem was to protect the high Himalayan Bhutanese border from incursions by the PRC. In this matter India received the cooperation of the Royal Government. However, the King's Prime Minister, Jigme Dorji, who supported alignment with India more often than a Nepal-style non-alignment between India and the PRC was assassinated in April, 1964. Dorji's younger brother, Lhendup Dorji, succeeded as acting Prime Minister but could not sustain his position because of the turmoil in the kingdom and the feelings among some of the elites against India. Lhendup Dorji, fearing for his life, fled to India shortly after the attempt on the King in July, 1965. Into all this was thrown Nari Rustomji, a friend of Jigme Dorji, as "Indian Adviser" in 1963. Due however to the confused situation in elite circles, Rustomji was transferred in 1966.

Bhutan, with India's cooperation, followed a gradual expansion of relations with states acceptable to India. It obtained membership in the United Nations in 1971 and joined the Non-Aligned Movement (NAM) in 1979. Despite occasional strains in their relationship, Bhutan continues to receive Indian economic aid and guidance on foreign policy. Bhutan can be described as an independent state enjoying Indian protection; it is not an Indian protectorate.

In the case of Nepal, Nehru preferred to have the kingdom walk a tight rope in its relations with India and the PRC and to act as a buffer zone when it suited India's security interests. The Indo-Nepali Treaty of 1950 provided for mutual consultation in the event of Nepal or Sikkim being threatened by an outside power. The treaty with Nepal was signed because of the PRC's claim to her "traditional boundarties" which in unofficial Chinese government statements included Bhutan, Sikkim, Nepal and Tibet.[7]

This "special relationship" was maintained between the two states (India and Nepal) until 1955 when the relationship suffered a strain. King Mahendra, who ascended the throne in 1955, had to cope with Nepali criticism that India was increasingly influencing Nepal's external relations and that Nepal's sovereign status had thereby been compromised. Mahendra decided to balance off the opposition to India by entering into diplomatic relations with the PRC in August, 1955. The PRC provided economic aid to Nepal, The PRC Prime Minister, Chou En-lai, visited Khatmandhu in January, 1957 and April, 1960. India too provided economic aid to Nepal. However, India refrained from protesting against King Mahendra's affiliations with the PRC. There was deterioration in Sino-Indian relations in regard to the border and it was not in India's interests to precipitate matters.

Between 1958-59, the Indian National Congress's parallel organisation, the Nepali National Congress, exerted pressure on King Mahendra. The King then held an election in early 1959. B. P. Koirala, head of the winning Nepali Congress, was appointed Prime Minister. Koirala's position towards India would have softened, but he held office only until 15 December, 1960 when the King dismissed him and assumed all powers to himself. Mahendra reassured India and the PRC that he would maintain a neutral stance in Sino-Indian relations, which he did till his death in January, 1972. With the new king, Birendra, India utilised the distribution of river waters to keep Nepal in line. India entered into a bilateral agreement with Nepal in 1984 under which it would build 50 water schemes for that country. The leverage of water inhibits Nepal from pursuing policies not appropriate for India. The position now is that King Birendra has stated that his kingdom is not part of the subcontinent. It "belonged to that part of Asia which touched both China and India".[8] King Birendra thus successfully used the hostile relations between India and the PRC to secure for his country a position which temporarily released him from excessive pressure from its two giant neighbours. Nepal, in the final analysis, has to follow New Delhi's dictates because of her economic dependence on India. Four to five million Nepalis are reported to work permanently in India in addition to 100,000 seasonal Nepali migrant workers who cross the Indo-Nepali border each year.[9]

Sri Lanka ("Ceylon", at the time, until 1972 when the island state's name was changed) from independence (1948) to 1956 adopted a foreign policy distinctly fearful of India. The island was internally stable and was not therefore a portentous threat to India. India intervened only when the Sinhalese-Tamil conflict reached the proportions of a major civil war after the anti-Tamil riots of July, 1983.

Before the grant of independence by Britain, Ceylon's leader, Don Stephen Senanayake, negotiated a defence agreement with Britain (November, 1947). The agreement permitted British military bases in the island in return for Britain agreeing to come to Ceylon's assistance in the event of attack. India did not consider British bases a threat. Ceylon and India are members of the Commonwealth and India enjoys pride of place in the New

Commonwealth. The Commonwealth association, for Nehru, was a platform to communicate with the world.

Nonetheless Ceylon's first Prime Minister, Don Stephen Senanayake, stated in April, 1949 that there was "an undercurrent of apprehension regarding the long-term possibility of Indian expansion."[10] Senanayake's constitutional advisor, Sir Ivor Jennings, wrote in April, 1956 that the Prime Minister was at the time of independence "well aware" of the danger that "India under the wrong leadership" could become "aggressive".[11] Sir John Kotelawala (Prime Minister, 1953-56) caused some anxiety to Krishna Menon at the Bandung Conference of 1955 and thereafter when for a fleeting period the idea of Ceylon joining the South-East Asia Treaty organisation (SEATO) was considered.[12]

An uncertain feeling towards India persisted despite the change in government in 1956 and the formulation of a policy of "dynamic neutralism" by the new Prime Minister, S. W. R. D. Bandaranaike.[13] This policy change implied Ceylon's involvement in the Non-Aligned Movement.

But the basic uncertainty remained among Ceylon's political elites and was reflected in their expressed fears of India. In 1955, S. W. R. D. Bandaranaike, leader of the Opposition and founder-leader of the Sri Lanka Freedom Party (SLFP), soon to become Prime Minister (1956) stated in a debate on the subject of making Sinhala the only state language:[14]

> I believe there are not inconsiderable numbers of Tamils in this country out of a population of eight million. Then there are forty to fifty million people just adjoining, and what about all this Tamil literature, Tamil teachers, even the films, papers, magazines, so that the Tamils in our country are not restricted to the Northern and Eastern provinces alone; there are (*sic*) a large number, I suppose over ten lakhs in Sinhalese provinces. And what about the Indian labourers whose return to India is now just fading into the dim and distant future? The fact that in the towns and villages, in business-houses and boutiques, most of the work is in the hands of Tamil-speaking people will inevitably result in a fear, and I do not think an unjustified fear, of the inexorable shrinking of the Sinhalese Language ...

In October 1956, J. R. Jayewardene, then a leading Opposisional spokesman of the defeated United National Party (UNP) censured the change to neutralism alleging that "leading Indians were saying that India should occupy Trincomalee when the British moved out."[15] All this, despite Nehru's assurances in 1950 and 1959 that India had no intention of "absorbing Ceylon".[16]

The policy of dynamic neutralism was actively maintained by S. W. R. D. Bandaranaike's widow during the phases when she was Prime Minister, 1960-65 and 1970-77. But even with the Bandaranaikes there was a fear of India. One reason was the developing ties between discontented Ceylon Tamils and Tamil political leaders in Tamil Nad. Felix Dias Bandaranaike who was Mrs. Sirimavo Bandaranaike's principal cabinet advisor remarked, in private conversation, that his government would call on the PRC for assistance if an Indian attack materialised.

These reservations notwithstanding, the Indian Prime Minister, Nehru, sent the foremost Catholic dignitary in India, Cardinal Valerian Gracias, to mediate in the dispute between the Catholic Church in Ceylon and Mrs. Bandaranaike over her government's decision to nationalise all schools, the majority of which were owned by the Church. The deadlock created a major crisis for the SLFP governement of the time. In 1971, Mrs. Indira Gandhi assisted Mrs. Bandaranaike in bringing under control the insurrection of the ultra-Marxist People's Liberation Front (the JVP) which at times seemed to overwhelm government forces. Thus India was ready to help Ceylon whenever domestic chaos threatened to upset the equilibrium.

Mrs. Bandaranaike's occasionally independent foreign policy stances did not affect India's security interests. During her first phase, 1960-65, she functioned as an intermediary between India and the PRC on their border dispute. Her efforts brought no results but was appreciated by the governments of both states. The exercise gave the PRC an opportunity of improving relations with Ceylon. In 1971, in the Bangladesh crisis, Mrs. Bandaranaike declared Ceylon's strict neutrality. Nevertheless, Pakistan's aircraft were permitted stopovers and refuelling rights at Ceylon's Bandaranaike airport en route from Pakistan to Dhaka. (India had banned such flights over Indian territory). The decision did not strain Indo-Ceylon relations.

Even President J. R. Jayewardene's pro-West foreign policy and his government's progressive alienation from the NAM did not irritate India to the point of interference. However, the growing conflict between Sinhalese and Tamils increasingly destabilised the island's policy and caused concern in Tamil Nad, a relevant political constituency for Rajiv Gandhi's government. The last straw was the intervention of hostile and unfriendly foreign powers (to India) and their agents in the Island's affairs, especially during 1983-87. The grant of facilities to the Voice of America which it was feared would broadcast messages at low frequency levels to U.S. nuclear submarines deep in the bottom of the North Indian Ocean could have caused concern to the USSR and therefore to India. Article 8 of the Indo-Soviet Friendship Treaty of August, 1971 required either side to prevent the use of its territory for military purposes that might be detrimental to the other side (for this purpose, it is probable that the USSR regarded Ceylon as part of the Indian sphere of influence). Article 9 reinforces Article 8 when it stipulates that in order to ensure that neither side will assist a third party (probably the PRC or U.S.A.) taking part in an armed conflict with the other side, the two parties (the USSR and India) will eliminate this threat and ensure the peace and security of their countries.[17]

The situation was made worse when President Jayewardene obtained the services of Pakistani, Israeli and British (unofficial) military advisors and arms from the Republic of South Africa. He claimed that he required foreign military assistance to quell the insurgency of the Tamil Freedom Fighters. Foreign involvement and the gradual engulfment of the island in a deleterious civil war compelled India to enter the scene first as a mediator (1983-7) and, later, militarily in 1987.[18] India's intervention was not part of a hegemonistic design or an implementation of Mrs. Indira Gandhi's alleged version of a Monroe Doctrine for South Asia, as various commentators speculated. Rajiv Gandhi's action in 1987, on the contrary, was in total agreement with the policy on Nepal spelled out by his grandfather, Jawaharlal Nehru in January, 1950.[19]

In 1983-4, Mrs. Gandhi sent her Minister for Foreign Affairs, Narasimha Rao, and the Chairman of her Policy Planning Committee, (who had membership in the Indian cabinet as well) G. Parthasarathy, to investigate and seek resolution of the Sinhalese-Tamil conflict. President Jayewardene's relationship with Parthasarathy was far from cordial as indicated by the President to me in October, 1983. Nor was the President willing to be persuaded by Mrs. Gandhi. I met with President Jayewardene in London in mid-1984 shortly after his visit to President Reagan. The President did not seem hopeful of the results of his talks in the White House. But he was also hesitant when I urged him, before his visit to Mrs. Gandhi, to use her good offices to settle the increasingly rough civil war. Mrs. Gandhi, from my own reliable sources, did not trust the President. Had President Jayewardene accepted G. Parthasarathy's Annexure 'C' formula as a solution to the Sinhalese-Tamil problem, Mrs. Gandhi would probably have insisted that her government monitor its implementation.

After Mrs. Gandhi'a assassination, her successor, Rajiv Gandhi, tried from 1984 to July, 1987 without success to resolve the issue. Gandhi's foreign secretary, Romesh Bhandari, and his cabinet minister (of state), P. Chidambaram,failed to get the two parties to agree to a mediated settlement. Failure resulted in Rajiv Gandhi himself negotiating the Indo-Sri Lanka Accord of 29 July, 1987. The Accord secured the Sri Lanka government's commitment to an Indian-devised peace plan which would end the civil war. President Jayewardene, more importantly, in letters of exchange annexed to the Accord, agreed to terminate the services of foreign military personnel and ensure Trincomalee as a harbour over which India would have prior participation-involvement. India committed itself to guarantee "the territorial integrity and unity" of Sri Lanka. Thus Indian intervention in the end provided for the safeguarding of India's vital interests; it was also an attempt at restoring equilibrium in the Sinhalese-Tamil conflict.

On the resolution of the Sinhalese-Tamil problem, Rajiv Gandhi frequently consulted with Tamil Nad's Chief Minister at the time, M. G. Ramachandran (deceased December, 1987). Tamil Nad was an important constituency for the Rajiv Gandhi government. The Accord did not bring the results expected. Sri Lanka's problems have in fact become aggravated because of Sinhala displeasure with the Indian military presence and the opposition to the Indian Peace Keeping Force (IPKF) from the principal Tamil group of freedom fighters, the Liberation Tigers of Tamil Eelam (LTTE).

President Jayewardene himself aggravated the situation by his unwise pronouncements. He failed to placate moderate Tamil opinion thereby polarising Sinhalese and Tamils. He was most impolitic in his views on Mrs. Gandhi and on the Kashmir issue. In his state visit to New Delhi in 1978 as the guest of the government of Morarji Desai (1977-9), President Jayewardene referred undiplomatically to Mrs. Gandhi's "undemocratic" period of emergency rule. When I told him on his return that the statement would be taken amiss by Mrs. Gandhi, President Jayewardene said he was confident that the Desai government had come to stay (a wrong political projection). On 27 August, 1979 in a letter to the convenor of the Tamil Co-ordinating Committee in London (K. Vaikunthavasan), Mrs. Gandhi wrote

> I ... am horrified to see the enclosures.
>
> The Janata Party Government (of Morarji Desai) is going out of its way to be friendly with the present government of Sri Lanka. I doubt if they will wish to take up the issue of the sufferings of the Tamils in Sri Lanka. At the moment all attention is on our election but I shall see if it is possible to bring this issue to the notice of the public in some other way.[20]

President Jayewardene was just as lacking in political sagacity in visiting General Zia Ul-Huq in Islamabad in April 1985. I asked him on the phone from Canada why he visited Pakistan when India was assisting him in seeking a resolution of his domestic crisis. His cryptic reply was "Why shouldn't I?" The President acted more unwisely in raising the issue of Jammu and Kashmir with General Zia. The Indian Prime Minister expressed concern, adding "we were disturbed that he (President Jayewardene) opened the Kashmir issue". The President's actions (on Mrs. Gandhi's emergency rule and Kashmir) were a blunder. His statement was an example of a powerless neighbour inviting to itself the needless hostility of political formations in the powerful neighbour-state.

Ceylon's leaders by and large had no concept of foreign policy goals. The emphasis since independence has centred on foreign aid. The Senanayakes (Don Stephen and Dudley) maintained the colonial attitude of reliance on Britain. S. W. R. D. Bandaranaike probably thought that involvement in the NAM would give him a platform on the world stage. Beyond this goal, he did little to restructure the foreign policy establishment or to formulate a strategy in terms of a world view. I had discussions along with a colleague (Professor S. U. Kodikara) of the University of Ceylon (now the University of Peradeniya) with the Prime Minister on inaugurating a Ceylon Institute of World Affairs (CIWA).[21] The Prime Minister gave encouragement and participated in the inaugural meeting of the CIWA. He did not, however, indicate any more interest in the progress and development of CIWA which to this day remains where it started in 1957.

Mrs. Sirimavo Bandaranaike's involvement on the world stage was more for domestic prestige. She lacks understanding of foreign policy orientations. At the meeting of Commonwealth leaders in 1961, she vigorously protested the South African application to remain in the Commonwealth after South Africa legislated for republican status. *The Times* (London) sardonically remarked that Mrs. Bandaranaike read from reams of typed sheets supplied to her by her cabinet confidant and advisor, Felix Dias Bandaranaike. Mrs. Bandaranaike's role in 1962 as intermediary in the aftermath of the Sino-Indian border war of 1962 was of little significance. Her attempt to have the Indian Ocean declared a zone of peace at the U.N. General Assembly in 1971 gave her marginal exposure, the Indian delegation undertaking most of the groundwork. Though Mrs. Bandaranaike received the plaudits of the more radical members of the NAM for her role in the Movement's progress, her policy orientations were not part of a coherent pattern.

In the case of Bangladesh too, Mrs. Gandhi did nothing more than follow her father's (Nehru) policy of safeguarding India's vital interests, or as a recent commentator remarked (in 1986), "of Indian interests".[22] This commentator, S. M. Mujtaba Razvi, described Mrs. Gandhi's policy as her version of a "Monroe Doctrine" in South Asia.[23] However, our view is that Mrs. Gandhi was keeping to the policy enunciated by Nehru in 1950 (on Nepal) though in a more difficult context. Razvi stated that Mrs. Gandhi described South Asia as "a troubled region" and he analysed Mrs. Gandhi's doctrine on "Indian interests" thus:

> The idea behind this doctrine was that if law and order breaks down in any South Asian state, it should seek India's help to overcome destabilization, or solicit help from within the region but not to the exclusion of India.[24]

This view on policy is not different from that of Nehru's case for intervening in Nepal should political chaos have overtaken that kingdom.

It was in these circumstances that Mrs. Gandhi intervened in East Pakistan. In order to ward off a possible threat from the PRC, Mrs. Gandhi took the precaution of concluding a mutual assistance pact with the Soviet Union, known as the Indo-Soviet Friendship Treaty of August, 1972. The decision to assist Mujibur Rahman in the creation of the state of Bangladesh had probably more to do with maintaining the stability of the South Asian system than this pact.

India's relations with Bangladesh have been based on the lever of riparian rights with Mrs. Gandhi's alleged Monroe doctrine coming into play from time to time.[25] The first ruler, Mujibur Rahman, had a satisfactory relationship. He was of course beholden to the Prime Minister. Mrs. Gandhi had assisted in the training and equipping of some 40,000 of Mujibur Rahman's own troops, the Mukti Bahini guerrillas. They played an important role in disrupting communications within Bangladesh, making it thereby easier for General Sam Manekshaw and his Indian forces to defeat Pakistan's armies.

Bangladesh started with good intentions, emulating the example of her secular neighbour and declaring herself the "People's Republic of Bangladesh". Within four years, Bangladesh developed troubles with India over the distribution of the waters of the two eastern rivers, the Ganges and the Brahmaputra. Then a coup finally brought General Ziaur Rahman firmly into power, at least for a while, in November, 1975.

General Rahman began a policy of distancing himself from New Delhi. One of his first acts was to sever any prospect of cultural cooperation. In 1978, he re-named the republic, "the Islamic Republic of Bangladesh." He emphasised *Bangladeshi* nationalism; he developed closer ties with Pakistan. Surjit Mansingh wrote in 1984 that from New Delhi's observations, "Bangladeshi officials gained the reputation of being the toughest, most demanding and most sensitive of all national groups with whom the Indian government has regular dealings."[26]

Internal destabilization of Rahman's regime now began. So up to the general elections of 1977 when Mrs. Gandhi suffered defeat at the hands of the Janata Party led by Morarji Desai, guerrilla raids on Bangladeshi territory were launched from Indian bases. Acts of internal sabotage were attributed to Indian *agents provocateur*. In the brief period 1977-9, when Desai was Prime Minister, Indo-Bangladesh relations improved. A five-year agreement was signed on 5 November, 1977 under which Bangladesh was guaranteed a sufficiency of water during the dry months. But this was atypical of Indian external policy as moulded by the Nehru-Gandhi Prime Ministerships.

In June, 1981 Lieutenant General H. M. Ershad took power after the assassination of General Ziaur Rahman and the failure of another coup soon thereafter. General Ershad and India signed the Indo-Bangladesh Accord of 31 May, 1984 but the evidence suggests that the relations between the two countries were not in equilibrium. There was a dispute over how the waters of the two rivers, the Ganges and the Brahmaputra, should be distributed so that Bangladesh will not suffer. The Indian occupation of Purbasha Island in the Bay of Bengal to which Bangladesh laid claims has been construed as an ill-considered act towards Bangladesh's claims over that island. India has protested against the outflow of Muslim immigrants from Bangladesh to the Indian state of Assam. India's attempts to construct a barbed wire fence along the Bangladesh-Assam border as a way of controlling immigration has added to General Ershad's discomfiture. Bangladesh's problem is to emphasize its independence from India's beneficence. To accomplish this objective Bangladesh has sought to establish a separate Islamic identity. This leaves Bangladesh looking for example, to Pakistan for Islamic and emotional support. Ziaur Rahman's government obtained aid from the US, the World Bank and Saudi Arabia and pro-Pakistani elements were, much to India's embarrassment, re-inducted into the Bangladeshi government. Bangladesh will, in the final analysis, be obliged to refrain from actions which will affect Indian interests. The leverage of water and India's superior military strength leaves Bangladesh with little or no option.

Pakistan's External Relations

Resentment against India is rooted in Pakistan's foreign policy goals. The immediate post-partition problems, including Kashmir, are not the only causes. Pakistan has been a state in search of a national identity. Pakistan seeks reinforcement of its presence in the Indian subcontinent by challenging India's position as the dominant power.

This seems irrational. India has a larger Muslim population than Pakistan. While Pakistan emphasises its Islamic identity, India maintains its secular character. India has 72 per cent of the land area of the subcontinent and 77 per cent of the population. Its sheer size and wealth in natural resources give India automatic pride of place. Nevertheless Pakistan's goal orientations have been directed at destabilising the Indian state system by, for example, encouraging the Khalistani Sikhs in their separatism, developing a nuclear profile and entering strategic treaty networks that are not consonant with Indian policies to avoid South Asia from being drawn into the power politics of states outside the region.

Pakistan seeks to be taken note of within South Asia. At the same time Pakistan has close ties with the United States and seeks a position of vantage in the Middle East system. Pakistan also maintains a relationship with the PRC as a counter to India. These policies have no impact on the other states of South Asia discussed here. The latter have not sought to enter Pakistan's foreign policy network. This unwillingness is partly to avoid discomfiting India. At the same time, with the exception of Bangladesh, the other states do not envisage any advantage for themselves in Pakistan's external commitments.

As early as in the period after independence, Pakistan's founder, Muhammad Ali Jinnah, decided in 1947 that it was necessary to protect the new state from Soviet aggression and "Hindu imperialism". Pakistan therefore looked for allies. In September 1948, Liaquat Ali Khan sent a secret message to the British Prime Minister, Clement Attlee. There was the suggestion of a military alliance between his country and Britain against communism. Communism, he stated, posed a danger to Pakistan's stability. Nothing definite emerged from this overture.[27] Then on 24 June, 1949, Liaquat Ali Khan told the British High Commissioner in Pakistan, L. B. Grafftey-Smith:

> What I fear is that Great Britain and the world would look on with folded arms if India attacked us.[28]

Britain did nothing to allay Pakistan's fears. Pakistan, therefore, in its search for security looked for allies to the Middle East, with the United States as an overall protector. The outcome was an agreement between Turkey and Pakistan on 19 February, 1954. There was provision for both parties to strengthen "peace and security in their own interest". On 19 May, 1954, Pakistan and the United States entered into a Mutual Defence Assistance Agreement. The U.S. agreed to provide military equipment and training to Pakistan's armed forces. Then followed the Manila Conference which resulted on 8 September, 1954 in the U.S. sponsored South-East Asia Collective Defence Treaty (SEATO). Pakistan was not satisfied with the provisions in the treaty. It did not arrange for a joint military command as in the case of

NATO. The U.S. added further disillusionment by writing in a reservation to the treaty: U.S. assistance would be provided only in the event of Communist aggression. Pakistan ratified the treaty on 19 January, 1955 but there was no guarantee that the U.S., Britain or France would come to Pakistan's aid in the event of an Indian attack.

Nor was the Baghdad Pact which Pakistan signed on 23 September, 1955 any more useful. Other signatories to this pact were Britain, Iraq, Turkey and Iran. The U.S., though a keen sponsor of the Pact, remained a non-signatory because of Israel. The point in question was the attitude of Arab states to Israel. When the U.S. joined the military committe of the Pact, the policy statement was again an assurance of protection against Communism, not against India. The British position was similar. Thus Pakistan's diplomacy in this phase had signally failed.

Pakistan's problem with India was the perceived aggression from that quarter, the troubles that followed partition and the dispute over Kashmir. At the start, Pakistan's Prime Minister, Liaquat Ali Khan, tried sorting out the post-partition problems with Nehru. On 8 April, 1950, Liaquat Ali Khan signed an agreement with Nehru which ended the fleeing of Hindus from East Pakistan to West Bengal and restricted Muslims leaving West Bengal for East Pakistan.

Earlier, contrary to his professed views on peaceful co-existence, Nehru had threatened in a speech in the Lok Sahba to use "other methods" against Pakistan on the question of Hindu refugees flowing into India.[29] After the Liaquat Ali Khan-Nehru Pact, Nehru stated: "We have stopped ourselves at the edge of the precipice and turned our back to it."[30]

In the following year, there followed the crises on Kashmir. In April 1951, the head of State in Kashmir issued a proclamation for the purpose of convening a constituent assembly. The assembly would decide "the future shape and affiliations of the state."[31] The *Economist* (25 August, 1951) reported that the assembly would carry out "its preordained part of formally voting for accession to India". India massed troops in East Punjab and Jammu and Kashmir.[32] Liaquat Ali Khan and his government prepared for the worst. The Pakistan army was far inferior in numbers and equipment to the Indians. The crisis passed.

Pakistan's inability to establish her military capabilities in the Indo-Pakistan war 1965, despite American military aid, marked a setback in the latter's bird for being a principal in the balance of power South Asia. A further setback followed with the dismemberment of the original state of Pakistan. In 1971, Bangladesh, with active Indian military assistance, seceded and became a state in its own right. Pakistan had hoped that the PRC and/or the U.S. would come to her assistance. Both powers failed her. The U.S. had provided military and economic aid to Pakistan. But the U.S. was helpful to India, too. Pakistan laid much hope in the People's Republic of China. But beyond protestations of support, encouragement and some military aid, China refrained. On 9 September, 1965, the Prime Minister of the People's

Republic, Chou En-lai, denounced India as the aggressor in the Indo-Pakistan war of September, 1965 and condemned the policies of "U.S. imperialism" and of "the modern revisionists" of the U.S.S.R.

On 23 September (1965) both states agreed to end the war. Pressure had been brought to bear on them by Britain and the United States. The Soviet Union called for a cessation of hostilities. On 10 January, 1966, as a result of Soviet initiatives, Pakistan's President Ayub Khan, and the Indian Prime Minister, Lal Bahadur Shastri, signed the Tashkent Agreement. The Agreement provided for a withdrawal by the two states to the borders they held prior to 5 August, 1965. There was dissatisfaction in both Indian and Pakistani circles to the concessions made by each party to the other. Shastri died of heart failure on 11 January, 1966 at Tashkent. What was serious to India was the Soviet attitude. The Soviet Union agreed to provide military aid to Pakistan. More ominous was the parity of treatment accorded to the two states by the USSR.

There was also the complicating factor of the PRC's involvement with Pakistan. The Sino-Pakistan relationship was negotiated by President Ayub's Foreign Minister, Zulfikar Bhutto (1963). Bhutto concluded a Sino-Pakistan Boundary Agreement on 2 March, 1963 under which large areas of northern Kashmir and Ladakh (disputed territory held by India) were recognised by Pakistan as belonging to China. By August 1963, Bhutto's diplomacy cemented the Sino-Pakistan relationship. Bhutto, however, failed to get the U.N. Security Council to discuss Kashmir, in part due to Nehru's death in 1964. In June 1966, Bhutto resigned from President Ayub's cabinet on medical grounds. He had however sensed the growing opposition to Ayub's regime. In particular, Pakistanis opposed the Tashkent Agreement as "a sellout" to India. With Shastri's death in January 1966, Pakistan had to deal with a more formidable foe and a skilled diplomatist in Mrs. Indira Gandhi.

Pakistan's policy towards India after the Bangladesh debacle has been one of open rancour. President Zia Ul-Huq had taken steps to (1) avoid Pakistan's encirclement, (2) safeguard Pakistan from a "menacing" India, and (3) strengthen the Islamic foundations of the state as a counter to what the Pakistanis think is an aggressive Hindu India.

President Zia had sought assistance from the PRC and the United States to break out of a possible Indo-Soviet encirclement. President Zia's policy had been to improve U.S. military ties with Pakistan, the excuse being that the U.S. needs bases in Pakistan to assist the Afghani Resistance against the Soviets in Afghanistan. However, U.S. aid to Pakistan is balanced off by U.S. assistance to India. The Pakistani government also continues to maintain military links with the PRC. To ensure easier border contact with the PRC, Pakistan has disputed India's claim to the world's highest glacier, Siachin.[33] India claims the glacier as part of Jammu and Kashmir. Siachin is a strategic link-up between Pakistan and China. New Delhi is concerned that this is one more instance of Sino-Pakistan military collaboration.

General Zia next tried, with a view to promoting Pakistan's image, to improve relations with the Arab states of the Middle East. In this again Pakistan's diplomacy was not successful. Pakistan's support for Britain in the Suez War (1956) had alienated Arab nationalists. To a large extent this was repaired when an Islamic Summit Conference was held in Lahore in 1974, during the Bhutto years. But the Conference which might have provided positive support to Pakistan in her problems with India failed to make headway because of Bhutto's personal ambitions to secure for himself the leadership of a Muslim bloc.

Pakistan also failed in her bid to establish closer relations with Iran. Whilst India had been a competitor, the Pakistanis are divided from the Iranians, sectwise, the former being Sunnis and the latter Shiites. Pakistan has closer ties with Saudi Arabia but the relationship is mainly on technical cooperation. Turkey and Iran have been lukewarm in supporting Pakistan under the CENTO agreement. Pakistan has thus had to depend wholly on U.S. military aid and PRC support.

The frustrated General Zia had a way out. This was to encourage Pakistan's scientific establishment's strenuous and persistent attempts to discover a nuclear device. India exploded a nuclear device in 1974 and halted attempts thereafter. The explosion was a response to the PRC, not to Pakistan. Recent reports indicate that Pakistan is close to testing a nuclear device. But this was after the failure of attempts by Pakistan to persuade India to sign a treaty, among other provisions of which were[34]

(1) renouncing the manufacture or acquisition of nuclear weapons, and
(2) an offer to join with India in a system of mutual inspection of all nuclear facilities in the two countries, on a bilateral basis.

The Indian Prime Minister declined to sign a Non-Nuclear Proliferation Treaty with General Zia at their Delhi Summit Meeting on 17 November, 1986. Both leaders however agreed not to attack each other's nuclear power installations. New Delhi does not accept General Zia's assurances to the UN General Assembly of "Pakistan's irrevocable commitment not to acquire nuclear explosive devices."[35] The Indian response is twofold:[36]

(1) Pakistan's proposals for joint inspections and safeguards are only to enable Pakistan to gain time for developing nuclear devices, and
(2) Pakistan's suggestion for a nuclear weapons zone in South Asia does not "take cognizance of Chinese nuclear capability."

India indeed has a valid point. The PRC as Pakistan's ally could always present a nuclear threat to India.

General Zia's third step was to strengthen the Islamic foundations of Pakistan. Ever since its creation, Pakistan has endeavoured to establish its identity by emphasising its Islamic character. Under General Zia, with Islamic fundamentalism rampant all over the Muslim world, it seemed politically rewarding to toe the line, and establish liaison with other Muslim states affected by Islamic fundamentalism. This could serve as a barrier to any attempt to bring Pakistan within India's orbit. Zia, therefore, declared that he would hold elections only after he was convinced that the future government would enforce the Islamic system. "Sovereignty", he added, "belonged to Allah ..."[37] From Pakistan's point of view, it was necessary for General Zia to enunciate this concept. With centrifugal forces encouraged by India and Soviet-backed Afghanistan there was need to consolidate the internal unity of a disparate country.

Pakistan also faces a threat from the 1000 miles of border with Afghanistan, the Durand Line as it came to be called. Pakistan's fear is that the pro-Soviet government in Afghanistan will encourage the Baluchi and Pushtun secessionist movements. The pro-Soviet President of Afghanistan promised support for the legitimate aspirations of the Baluchis and Pushtuns.

The South Asian Association for Regional Cooperation (SAARC)

The group of seven (India, Pakistan, Bangladesh, Sri Lanka, Nepal, Bhutan and the Maldives) met formally in 1981 and have had several meetings since. The model is ASEAN. President J. R. Jayewardene told me that he and his Prime Minister(R. Premadasa) had made every effort to seek admission to ASEAN. But Lee Kuan Yew (Prime Minister of Singapore) whilst sympathetic to Sri Lanka's aspirations, cautioned the Sri Lanka government that geographic location would be the factor against Sri Lanka obtaining membership. The point in all this is that Sri Lanka did not like being involved in SAARC where Indian dominance would prevail.

With a dominant power such as India and the ongoing conflict between the latter and Pakistan, there is more likely to be bilateral cooperation between states rather than the group converting itself into an economic community. Some members of the group have had their sovereignties curtailed by India (Sri Lanka and Bhutan). Others are economically vassals of India (the Maldives) or landlocked and dependent on India (Nepal). The SAARC is for trade, not a political forum. But extraneous issues such as terrorism have been raised at meetings whereas the principal objective is to promote economic cooperation. Even in this field, cooperation is to be in selected areas of cultural and economic activities. Cooperation does not cover a wide range, the targeted areas being subjects such as agricultural development, rural development, telecommunications, meteorology and health care. SAARC will probably grow in time. The main obstacles are the disputes between members.

Conclusions

One of the problems of South Asia is that for international purposes, it is not regarded as a subsystem. If it were a subsystem, it would become the task of the international community to ensure its stability and equilibrium and give due weight to opinions expressed by its leaders. This does not happen. India is the only state where personalities such as Nehru and Mrs. Indira Gandhi were reckoned with. But a subsystem must also be a cohesive bloc. South Asia does not function as one. This is because of India's desire to safeguard her vital interests and Pakistan's fear of Indian "expansionism"; also Pakistan has an urge to challenge India's desire to be militarily strong. There is no documentation to prove the case but South Asia, in our view, has become a troubled region where foreign powers cast their nets.

The PRC does not wish India to emerge as the supreme power. Hence its support to Islamabad and its attempts to establish closer ties with Bangladesh and Nepal. The PRC is interested in the happenings in Sri Lanka. The PRC ambassador told me in Colombo, in 1979, that his country would help in every way to resolve the ethnic problem but would try to prevent the island becoming two separate states. When I asked him for his reason, he stated that two ministates would become a prey to Soviet machinations and that Sri Lanka lay in the sea lanes from the PRC to the African states. Thus the PRC poses an obstacle to the emergence of a subsystem.

There have always been rumours of U.S. involvement. Certainly, during the period 1977-84 when I advised President Jayewardene and was the intermediary between the President and the Tamil United Liberation Front (TULF), I was in frequent contact with the U.S. ambassador in Colombo.[38] He was only interested in peace and normalcy. There was no hint of a U.S. presence even tangentially. President Jayewardene himself did not look on the U.S. as an ally; more as an aid-giver. But the U.S. involvement in Pakistan again interferes with subsystemic development.

The High Commissioner for India in Ceylon did not express any Indian desire to possess the island. He was keen that there should be a resolution of the conflict. He discounted the idea of the Tamil areas effecting an "enosis" with Tamil Nadu. It was the same with G. Parthasarathy when I met him in New York in October, 1983. He ruled out the possibility of any kind of Indian military intervention. Our conclusion is that India intervened in Sri Lanka because there was no possibility of persuading President Jayewardene and his government to implement even the modest undertakings they proposed for Tamil autonomy.

The fact that India is, since 1971, allied to the USSR does not alter the situation. There is no validity to support the view that India is "a client state" of the USSR. The pact is one of mutual assistance and was obviously intended to protect India against full-scale PRC aggresion. Nevertheless the USSR connection, once more, creates a problem for the formation of a subsystem.

There is also the view that the PRC looks on India as a rival in the world system. The PRC seeks the status of an "alternationist power" to challenge the duopoly of the planet exercised by the two superpowers. In our view, the PRC's main preoccupation is to get her borders straight with India. Nepal and Bhutan are relevant in this exercise. Bangladesh and Sri Lanka touch on Indian interests and are therefore within India's strategic sphere of interest.

The risk is in the superpowers and foreign middle powers fishing in the troubled waters of fissiparous tendencies in the body politic of some of the states of South Asia; not only foreign powers but neighbouring states as well.

This could cause civil wars within states; an opportunity for armament dealers and for interested powers to carry out their objectives is presented. A wiser statesmanship is called for. There can be no military solutions to ethnic problems as post-World War II examples (with the exception of the state of Israel) indicate. If that statesmanship is not forthcoming, the United Nations will have to intervene so that the nations at war within the state will end their feuding and submit their dispute to a neutral organisation. That is why we suggest that South Asia be looked upon as a subsystem of the international community. Intervention or inquiry into troubled regions would then become compelling.

NOTES

1 Quoted by Leo Rose in his "Bhutan's External Relations", *Pacific Affairs*, Vol. 47, No. 2 (Summer 1974), P. 194; for an overall view, see Ashok Kapur, "Indian Foreign Policy: Perspectives and Present Predicament", *The Round Table*, No. 295, July 1985, pp. 230-39.
2 Rose, *ibid.*
3 Bharat Wariavwalla, "Indira's India: A National Security State?" *The Round Table* (1983), 287, p. 282.
4 Leo E. Rose and Margaret Fisher, *The Politics of Nepal: Persistence and Change in an Asian Monarchy* (Ithaca, 1970), pp. 122-3.
5 For these and other details see Surjit Mansingh, *India's Search For Power: Indira Gandhi's Foreign Policy 1966-1982*, pp. 282-3 and "Asianism" in Sudershan Chawla, *The Foreign Relations of India* (California and Belmont, 1976), pp. 52-55, 121.
6 Leo E. Rose and Margaret Fisher, p. 150, footnote 4.
7 For further information, refer to Leo. E. Rose, *Pacific Affairs*, Vol. 47, No. 2; the information that follows on Rustomji, the Dorjis and developments in Bhutan is from Rose, *ibid.*
8 See Leo Rose, *Nepal: Strategy for Survival* (London, 1971), p. 280; also S. M. Mujtaba Razvi, "Conflict and Cooperation in South Asia", *The Round Table*, No. 299, July 1986, p. 276.
9 Surjit Mansingh, *India's Search For Power: Indira Gandhi's Foreign Policy 1966-1982* (New Delhi/Beverley Hills/London, 1984), p. 287.
10 Quoted by T. A. Keenleyside, "Nationalist Indian Attitudes Towards Asia: A Troublesome Legacy for Post-Independence Indian Foreign Policy", *Pacific Affairs*, 55(2), Summer 1982, pp. 228-9.
11 In "Crown and Commonwealth in Asia", *International Affairs* (London), 32: 138, April 1956.
12 See Sir John Kotelawala, *An Asian Prime Minister's Story* (London, 1956).
13 For an exposition of "Dynamic neutralism" under the title "Neutralism and Cowardice", see *The Foreign Policy of Ceylon: Extracts From Statements By The Late Prime Minister, Mr. S. W. R. D. Bandaranaike and Texts of Joint Statements issued by him and Visiting Heads of State* (Colombo 1961, revised and enlarged) pp. 10-11.
14 *Parliamentary Debates* (House of Representatives), Vol. 23, column 684.
15 *The Times* (Ceylon), 2 October, 1956.
16 At the Commonwealth Foreign Ministers' Conference in Colombo in January 1950, *Ceylon Daily News*, 16 January, 1950 and again in 1959, see S. U. Kodikara, *Indo-Ceylon Relations Since Independence* (Colombo, 1965), p. 21.
17 The full text of the Treaty is in Appendix C, Mansingh, pp. 387-9.
18 For the stages of India's involvement before the Indo-Sri Lanka Accord, see my *The Break-up of Sri Lanka: The Sinhalese-Tamil Conflict* (Honolulu, 1988).

19 For the full text of the Indo-Sri Lanka Accord, see *Tamil Times*, August 1987 (Vol. VI, No. 10).
20 This letter was given to me by K. Vaikunthavasan for perusal.
21 I was at that time a faculty member in political science, Department of Economics, University of Ceylon and S. U. Kodikara was from the Department of History. Kodikara had at that time specialised in Indo-Ceylon Relations which dealt with the decitizenised Indian plantation workers.
22 Razvi, *ibid.*, p. 274.
23 *Ibid.*
24 *Ibid.*
25 The information that follows on Bangaladesh is derived from S. M. Mujtaba Razvi, *op. cit.*, and Surjit Mansingh, *op. cit.*
26 Surjit Mansingh, p. 269.
27 Anita Inder Singh, "Post-Imperial British Attitudes to India: The Military Aspect, 1947-51", *The Round Table*, No. 296, October 1985, p. 365.
28 *Ibid.*
29 S. M. Burke, *Pakistan's Foreign Policy: An Historical Analysis* (London, 1973), p. 57.
30 *Op. cit.*, p. 58.
31 *Loc. cit.*, p. 59.
32 Nehru's position on Kashmir was that: "as far as we are concerned, it is desirable for us from a strategic point of view that Kashmir should be with us"; quoted by A. P. Rana, *The Imperatives of Non-Alignment: A Conceptual Study of India's Foreign Policy Strategy in the Nehru Period* (Delhi, 1976), p. 34.
33 Razvi, p. 271.
34 *Ibid.*, p. 270.
35 General Zia is quoted by Ravzi, *ibid.*, p. 271.
36 *Ibid.*, also Ashok Kapur, "Nuclear Proliferation: South Asian Perspectives" (Review Article), *Pacific Affairs*, Vol. 57 (2) Summmer 1984, pp. 304-10.
37 See Ataur Rahman "Pakistan: Unity or Further Divisions" in A. Jeyaratnam Wilson and Dennis Dalton (eds.) *The States of South Asia* (London, 1982), p. 205.
38 See my "Racial Strife in Sri Lanka: The Role of an Intermediary" in *Conflict Quarterly* (University of New Brunswick), Spring-Summer, 1982.

Japan: Diplomacy of a Developmental State

ROBERT E. BEDESKI*

ABSTRACT

In the last century, Japanese diplomacy has been the lesser partner of two major forces arising out of her remarkably rapid modernization—military expansion and economic growth. In the first period, geographical propinquity and imperial ambitions led to aggrandizement at the expense of continental neighbors. Since 1945, Japanese diplomacy has aimed at maintaining friendly relations with all trading partners and at upholding the international environment which has been so conducive to the nation's economic growth. The Security Treaty with the US has enabled Japan to maintain a minimum armed force, but pressures are mounting to expand defense spending.

JAPAN HAS PLAYED two major power roles—military, until 1945; and economic, since the 1960s. In the first case, the outcome was disaster and devastation, and in the second, Japan has become one of the most economically advanced societies in human history. The nation has demonstrated the ability of a relatively small and resource-poor people to develop in a hurry, overcome international obstacles, and become a major economic player in the contemporary world. The Japanese have been able to form a national consensus on developmental goals and pursue them with a dedication that has astonished the world. In this setting, diplomacy has been critical in adapting domestic developments to the international arena.

Seizaburo Sato listed the "principal attitudes characterizing the perceptions and preferences of both the elite and the attentive public toward the international environment over the past one hundred years" as "(1) a strong sense of belonging to Japan and the Japanese race, coupled with deep-rooted feelings of inferiority; (2) an intense concern with improving the country's international status; (3) a deep anxiety over being isolated internationally; (4) a desire to conform to world trends (*sekai no taisei*); and (5) an emotional commitment to Asia, which has resulted in a focusing of attention on that area".[1]

The Evolution of the Japanese State

Since the Meiji Restoration (1868), the Japanese have mobilized their human and meagre material resources to develop into a modern society.[2] The

* Department of Political Science, University of Victoria, Victoria, Canada.

example of China's decline and subjection to unequal treaties stimulated the Japanese to restructure their state and to modernize the legal system to establish full national sovereignty by 1900. With the signing of the 1894 Aoki-Kimberly Treaty, "Britain became the first power provisionally to renounce extraterritoriality". This was a "milestone in Japan's struggle to enter international society". Nevertheless, even after full treaty equality had been established, the other powers continued to discriminate against Japanese immigrants.[3] Japan had already flexed its military muscle in defeating the Chinese Empire in 1895 and had annexed Taiwan. In building an overseas empire, the Japanese were imitating the pattern of other industrialized countries, such as Great Britain. Rapid legal and military modernization facilitated acceptance of Japan as diplomatic equal, and not only were the unequal treaties abolished, but Britain entered into an alliance with Japan in 1902. "Japan emerged as both a non-European and a non-Christian power."

The treaty aimed to contain the Russian empire, and in 1904, Japan went to war and defeated the second great Asian empire. In 1910, Japan consolidated its foothold on the continent by annexing the kingdom of Korea. Revolutions and civil wars in China provided further opportunities to expand there. The dream of Toyotomi Hideyoshi to conquer the Ming empire in China[4] was revived. From 1931 through 1945, the imperial army and navy invaded China, then Southeast Asia.

The war and empire ended in 1945 in the nuclear holocausts of Hiroshima and Nagasaki. The military had taken control of the Japanese state and destroyed it. The conquest of empire had ruined Japan, and the country turned inward to rebuild. In the process of reconstruction, the US occupation provided a positive environment for rebuilding institutions and for modernization. The 1946 constitution, including the anti-war Article Nine, the dissolution of the *zaibatsu*, the land reform, and general liberalization of society eliminated many of the contradictions of pre-war Japan.[5]

Three Factors Which Have Influenced Japanese Diplomacy

Japanese diplomacy emerged from cultural isolation in the mid-nineteenth century. From Tokugawa enforcement of *sakoku* (closed nation) to demands for *sonno joi* (restore the emperor; expel the barbarians) to the building of a rich and powerful country,[6] Japan has continuously astounded the rest of the world. Few expected this feudal island kingdom to emerge as a major Pacific power—especially in the face of the seemingly overpowering presence of the Chinese empire.[7]

To more fully understand Japan's dynamism and impact on the region, three crucial factors will be considered: geopolitics, the international political environment, and developmentalism—a term derived from Chalmers Johnson discussion of Japan as a developmental state. This means that the state is "plan-rational", where the government gives "greatest precedence to industrial policy, that is to a concern with the structure of domestic industry and with promoting the structure that enhances the nation's international competitiveness."[8]

1. *Geopolitics*

Japan's geography has guided her destiny. Similar to Great Britain, Japan was exempt through much of its history from the great migrations and invasions which troubled the neighboring continent. The Chinese empire was in constant struggle with the various nomadic tribes and nations of central Asia. The closest the Japanese came to incorporation in the Chinese empire was when the Mongols launched two abortive invasions (1274 and 1281 AD) which were destroyed by the typhoons, or *shimpu*. (The other reading of this term, *kamikaze*, or "divine wind", became associated abroad with the suicide pilots in 1944 and 1945.) After the unification of the country in 1600, Portuguese and Dutch traders were restricted to an island in Nagasaki harbor. A period of peace and prosperity lasted through the Tokugawa Shogunate, and saw the emergence of trade, early capitalism, and the decline of feudalism under the centralizing government in Edo—modern Tokyo.

The Japanese have been close enough to the Asian continent to be aware of cultural currents, and to absorb Chinese lessons and institutions. But distance to the Asian mainland has been sufficient to make any borrowing a matter of choice. "...the historical isolation of Japan has been considerably greater than that of England. The widths of the straits separating each of these two island nations from the continent, about 115 miles for Japan, and only 21 miles for England, offer a good measure of the influence of geographical isolation on their respective histories."[9] The Taika reforms (646 AD) brought Confucian institutions—but not the meritocratic examination system—to Japan. The pattern of importing and adapting foreign institutions was well established when the country leadership decided to modernize in the Meiji period. Similar to the Russians, the Japanese culture was derived from an older and more sophisticated civilization than its own, and had few inhibitions about this borrowing. Japan had the advantage that water barriers allowed the leadership to control the introduction of foreign ideas, rather than to acquiesce in their involuntary diffusion.

If Belgium was the pistol aimed at the heart of Britain, then Korea was a dagger pointing at the heart of Japan. The Korean peninsula has been a major bridge from Japan to the continent. Buddhism and ceramics were among the imports, and modern Japanese can probably count a number of Koreans among their ancestors. Japanese rivalry with China and Russia on the Korean peninsula led to war with the first in 1894, and again with the Russian empire in 1904. After defeating the two largest empires in the world. Japan annexed Korea as a colony in 1910. In the 1930s the Korean bridgehead and the Manchurian railway gave the Japanese militarists a base from which to launch aggression against North China.

Another parallel between Japan and Russia was "their nineteenth-century response to Western military challenges, the process by which they sought to reconstruct values and institutions on the basis of European models... Also in the years between the world wars both countries saw the international system as essentially hostile to their interests, and were inclined to associate with and to draw assistance from a similarly alienated Germany—Russia particularly in the 1920s, Japan in the 1930s."[10]

Pre-war Japan viewed the East Asian region as one of crisis and opportunity. The specter of communism in the USSR—and its expansion into China—was claimed as justification for military action in North China. According to an apologist, "The recent Tokyo-Berlin-Rome Pact has set a new goal for mankind. Japan as the champion of East Asia, leading the crusade against communism, has a mission of vital significance in history. Only by beating back the Red tide surging from beyond China's Great Wall will it be possible to insure the peace of East Asia and to enable its peoples to continue on the road to civilization."[11] Although a member of the anti-Comintern Axis alliance, Tokyo refrained from attacking the USSR from the east—a move which would have further distracted the forces of Stalin. Occupying China and Southeast Asia, while fighting the US in the Pacific, was enough for the Japanese forces.

Japanese diplomacy and expansion on the Asian continent began shortly after 1868—the year of the accession of the Meiji emperor. As diplomats had claimed, "propinquity created special interests." This referred to Taiwan as well, which came under Japanese rule after the Treaty of Shimonoseki with China in 1895. Military and commercial interests moved hand-in-glove.

In World War One, Japan declared on the side of the Allied powers. It provided new opportunities for expansion. Japanese forces marched across the Shandong peninsula, ignoring Chinese sovereignty, and captured the German concessions there. German islands in the Pacific Ocean were also incorporated into the Japanese empire.

The dreams of empire were finding their horizons, and the Japanese diplomatic-military machine was providing the instruments for realizing those dreams. To the north were the Kuriles, Sakhalin and Siberia itself. After the Russian revolution, a Japanese expeditionary force had stayed in eastern Siberia as part of the larger Allied force, from 1918-1922.[12]

To the west was the Korean peninsula—the gateway to Manchuria and north China. To the south, was Okinawa, Taiwan and Southeast Asia. And to the east was the Pacific basin. As a late developing country, Japan demanded its own empire. Colonies seemed to be the necessary accessories for an industrial state. Far from the centers of Europe and North America, the East Asia-West Pacific region seemed to provide the natural Lebensraum for Japan.

2. *International Environment*

Relations with the US

Postwar Japan was stripped of its empire, and industry and its cities were left in ashes. The government was nearly totally discredited, and the conquerors felt justified in imposing severe punishment on Japan. The Emperor narrowly avoided prosecution as a war criminal because of his key role in the surrender, and his usefulness in facilitating the US occupation and the reforms.

The Japanese state was reconstituted under the 1946 constitution (promulgated in 1947) into a parliamentary democracy with a constitutional monarchy. Article Nine of the constitution outlawed war as a means of national policy and prohibited the establishment of a military force.[13] Although the prohibition remains, it has not prevented the development of the "Self Defense Forces", which operate under several restrictions but perform many of the same functions as other military forces. Similar to the Meiji Restoration, the US Occupation was a controlled revolution from above by an elite with a vision of Japan's future. In contrast to the first, however, the second revolution lacked constancy, was initiated and guided by a foreign government, and took place at a time when China was being transformed into a major communist power. The occupation began with the purpose of punishing Japan for being the aggressor in the Pacific war. The military was disbanded, and war crimes trials were held. As US-Soviet relations soured, and the Chinese communists gained the upper hand in the civil war, the US decided that a dependent, impoverished Japan was not in the best interests of regional security.

The Korean War was a catalyst making Japan the outpost of democracy and market capitalism in East Asia. A communist conquest of the Korean peninsula would have made the island nation a front line in the cold war, and removed US and Western influence from the East Asian mainland. The war accelerated the reindustrialization of the Japanese economy, and also reversed some of the more radical reforms of the institutions. The national police force was established, and leftist tendencies were thwarted.

The Korean war and its aftermath heightened the strategic importance of Japan to the security of East Asia.[14] Japan provided the logistical support and rear area for the UN action on the Korean peninsula. US army, naval and air bases provided for the strategic presence of the US after the occupation ended in 1951. At that time Japan signed a Treaty of Peace with most of the belligerents of World War Two—with the notable exception of the USSR and the People's Republic of China (PRC). A treaty was signed with the Republic of China on Taiwan.

The volatility of the region had not changed—only Japan's ability to intervene and affect those conflicts. From 1950 through 1975, the US was the dependable ally under the US-Japan Security Treaty to guarantee Japanese security. Under this arrangement, Japan was able to abide by the terms of its

Peace Constitution and limit defense spending to 1% of the Gross National Product. The Japanese policy of no nuclear weapons prohibited the US from deploying nuclear weapons in Japan. It was also understood to mean that US ships calling at Japanese ports would not carry such weapons. This restriction was breached a number of times, according to former US Ambassador Reischauer.

The US presence also had disadvantages. Japan, as the host of American bases, was a certain target in any nuclear exchange. It also meant that the country had less room for diplomatic choice since it so closely depended upon the US for defense. The US military presence, subordinate foreign policy, and gradual rearmament all provided issues for the opposition parties—led by the Japan Socialist Party. In 1960, opposition to the renewal of the Security Treaty and disgust with the way the government rammed it through the Diet led to the downfall of the Kishi government. Port visits by US carriers to its home port of Yokosuka near Tokyo have been greeted with demonstrations and protests.

During the premiership of Nakasone, relations with the US improved at a personal level with US President Reagan, but encountered difficulties in trade issues as the US deficit climbed ever higher. Speaking with more enthusiasm than discretion, the Prime Minister called Japan "an unsinkable aircraft carrier"—reminiscent of Britain in the Second World War. Angry reaction from domestic quarters forced him to qualify the statement. The metaphor was sensitive because it also fits into the context of current policy—for Japan to assume responsibility for security of shipping lanes within a radius of 1000 miles of Japan.[15]

Since 1975, the Japanese government has seen the US as a declining superpower. The withdrawal from Vietnam, the humiliation of the Teheran hostage affair, and President Jimmy Carter's plan to withdraw US troops from Korea were all symptoms of an overextended power which might not honor its commitments to Japanese security.[16] Prime Minister Ohira set up a committee to examine Japan's comprehensive security to deal with the question, but so far the government remains cautious about taking new initiatives which might disturb relations with the US.

Relations with the USSR

Contacts between the Russian empire and Japan began in the eighteenth century, and centered on the northern islands of Hokkaido, Sakhalin and the Kuriles. To prevent the Russian Pacific frontier from embracing Hokkaido, the Japanese government sent settlers there.

During the next century, Russian advances in Northeast Asia created friction in Korea and Manchuria, culminating in the 1904-1905 Russo-Japanese War. For the Russians, the war and its loss demonstrated several strategic lessons: First, the tenuous rail link to the east, the Trans-Siberian railway, was crucial in preserving the Pacific territories. It had been incomplete at the time of the war, and logistical support of the military forces against Japan faced considerable odds. Second, the stunning defeat of the Russian fleet in the Far East demonstrated the skills and competence of the new Japanese navy. Moreover, the Anglo-Japanese Treat of Alliance further complicated defense of the Russian Far East because the tsar's fleet could not pass through the Straits of Gibraltar or the Suez Canal, which were both controlled by the British. As a result, the Russian ships were forced to sail around the Cape of Good Hope, and arrived to battle the Japanese, poorly prepared after their seven month voyage. The fifty-odd ships of the former Baltic Fleet were decisively defeated.[17]

The Treaty of Portsmouth ceded northern Sakhalin and its lease of the Liaotung peninsula to Japan. The war was also a catalyst in the 1905 abortive revolution in Russia. In the space of a decade, the Japanese had severely wounded two huge and ancient empires—the Chinese and the Russian—demonstrating their feet of clay, and speeding their demise. Many Japanese accepted the doctrine of social Darwinism and saw their own destiny as that of a powerful and vigorous nation which had the right to expand at the expense of the old and corrupt empires.

Relations were re-established with the government in Moscow, but the two nations remained wary of one another. Tokyo saw the Soviets supporting the Communist Party of China as well as the Kuomintang (Guomindang) under Chiang Kai-shek (Jiang Jieshi). Militarists and right-wingers feared the Bolshevization of China which would roll back Japanese gains on the Asian continent and endanger Japan itself. Signing the anti-comintern pact with Germany and Italy formally obligated Japan to attack the USSR, but Tokyo failed to do this—allowing Stalin to concentrate most of his forces on the Western front.

In the final days of the war, Soviet forces entered Manchuria and the northern part of Korea and accepted the surrender of the Japanese forces. The Treaty of Yalta also gave Stalin control of the Kurile Islands. Subsequently the Japanese protested that this did not include the Northern Territories, and the issue remains a serious wedge between Japan and the USSR.

Relations with China

China, the other empire, had influenced Japan since at least the Tang dynasty. After borrowing language, religion and even concepts of city planning from the Chinese, Japan's contacts with the continent remained limited. Following the Second World War, Japan signed a peace treaty with Taiwan and maintained relations with the Taiwan Republic of China until 1972, when Prime Minister Tanaka travelled to Beijing and normalized relations between the two countries.[18]

At the time of normalization, Premier Zhou Enlai stated China's desire for a Treaty of Peace and Friendship, in order to further strengthen relations. Inclusion of the phrase "antihegemonism" in the draft treaty, however, alerted the Japanese to the anti-Soviet intent of the Treaty. "Hegemony" had become a code word in Chinese propaganda meaning Soviet expansionism, and following the death of Mao Zedong in September 1976, as well as the perceived decline of US military power in the wake of Vietnam, the Chinese were trying to build a coalition to redress the balance of power against the USSR. In 1977 and early 1978. China put increasing pressure on Japan to sign the treaty. Contracts for Japanese trade and investment to expand were signed, and the temptations to sign the Peace and Friendship Treaty were enormous.

While the mutual attractions were great, so were the potential costs. The PRC already had a Treaty of Alliance with the USSR, and it specifically mentioned the threat of Japan. It was due to expire in 1980, but during the period of signing the Peace and Friendship Treaty in August 1978, and the lapse of the Sino-Soviet Treaty, the Chinese were in a position of alliance against Japan in one treaty, and in a quasi-alliance with Japan in the second Treaty.

More important than the legal contradictions was the position of the USSR. Japan was already linked with the US under the Defense Treaty—which the Japanese officially deny is an alliance. When Japan signed the treaty containing anti-Soviet language, Moscow saw it as a preliminary step towards a US-Japan-PRC coalition. The Soviets vilified the Treaty as the modern version of the infamous anti-Comintern pact of Hitler. If the Japanese were gambling that the Treaty would pressure Moscow to compromise on the Northern Territories issue, their strategy backfired. More military forces and equipment were dispatched to the area, and Moscow increased assistance to Vietnam. It is likely that the Chinese diplomatic offensive, including not only the Peace and Friendship Treaty, but also normalization with the US, increased tensions in the region. It may be no coincidence that the Sino-Vietnam war of early 1979 and the Soviet invasion of Afghanistan—evidence of an escalating rivalry in the Asian region—occurred in the late 1970s following China's re-emergence as an international actor after the consolidation of Deng Xiaoping's position in late 1978.

Relations between China and Japan remain friendly, although the fortieth anniversary of the Marco Polo Bridge incident has rekindled old suspicions. The tendency towards greater defense spending in Japan—including the breaching of the 1% limit of the GNP—has also raised anxieties in various parts of East Asia.

3. *Developmentalism*

In his history of the Japan Ministry of International Trade and Industry (MITI), Chalmers Johnson refers to Japan as a "developmental state". In the postwar period, Japan's stress on economic growth and the self-denial of military expansion have played prominent roles in the formation of foreign policy. While export-led development has been important, Johnson sees the developmental orientation as crucial to the country's success.

In addition, a modernized version of Confucianism has spared Japan many of the distractions of more "liberal" democracies. The family, or *ie*, has provided some of the social security which other modern states have introduced in the welfare state. The notion of "entitlements" from the state remains relatively undeveloped, and environmental policy still lags behind that of other industrial nations. Stress on education has created a highly educated society, with a literate, skilled and flexible work force.

Japan has become one of the industrial superpowers of the present period, despite the necessity to import nearly all of its raw materials from abroad. To maintain this economic dynamism, diplomacy has remained as bland as possible. Conflict avoidance has been one of the key staples of Japanese foreign policy.

In late 1987, the government of South Korea requested that Japan play a mediating role in normalizing relations between Seoul and Beijing. Coming after the North Korean sabotage of the South Korean airliner in December, the Chinese were tempted to discipline an embarrassing ally. But a larger factor is that any formalization between the PRC and South Korea would probably increase Pyongyang's dependence on the USSR. In any event, an increasing Japanese role in the Korean peninsula is inevitable.

Since the early 1970s, with the Sino-Japanese normalization, Tokyo has been pursuing a slightly more independent foreign policy from the US. Overseas Development Assistance has significantly increased, and Japan remains committed to expanding this aid to developing countries.[19] In the two decades after the US-Japan Security Treaty, the pro-US orientation was a major source of dissent in the country. The opposition parties, chiefly the JSP, made resistance to US presence a major plank in its platform.

Although the LDP has been continuously in power since its formation in 1955, the anti-Security Treaty demonstrations of 1960 showed that it could not force its will on the Japanese people. Through slow and steady leadership, however, the government has been able to alter public opinion and create a rough consensus on foreign policy.

Conclusion

Japan emerged as a modern state unencumbered by a larger cultural community. Unlike the states of Europe, Japanese identity was not formed out of wars, alliances and invasions. Modernization has meant adoption of foreign institutions and adaptation to international standards. Unlike the Chinese, the burden of the past was not heavy, and ideology—except for the Emperor cult of pre-1945—has not overcome common sense.

The historical burden of war has been discarded with the help of an enlightened constitution and the Security Treaty with the US, allowing the country to pursue economic prosperity and technological excellence. The desire for peace, so widespread among the Japanese people, does not translate directly into its actuality. US-USSR confrontation and Japanese geography will not go away: "Japan stands on the most important route linking the Asian continent to the Pacific Ocean via the Sea of Okhotsk, the Sea of Japan, and the East China Sea which gives the country an important significance as a geographical point of contact between the continent and the ocean. This means that Japan's location is of great strategic importance to the U.S.-Soviet relationship of military confrontation across the Pacific Ocean."[20]

As economic growth continues, Japan faces increasing pressure to translate its wealth into greater military strength. Resentment in the US Congress calls for greater defense-burden sharing to relieve US costs. Any moves in this direction, however, set off alarms in Beijing, Jakarta, and other neighbors. The US is no longer the economic and military superpower of the postwar decades, and there have been increasing doubts concerning the American willingness to provide the full security expected under the Treaty. If another war erupts on the Korean peninsula, Japan may be faced with a painful choice of either allowing the north to conquer the south, or of intervening to maintain a historical buffer.

The task of Japanese diplomacy has been to navigate the nation through the dangers and opportunities of the international setting. As the US connection becomes more problematic, the old relationship of inequality between mentor and student is replaced by a partnership. Power in the modern world is far less concentrated than in earlier decades, and the Japanese envision a more active participation in international affairs than in the past post-war years.[21]

1 Seizaburo Sato, "The Foundations of Modern Japanese Foreign Policy," in Robert A. Scalapino (ed.): *The Foreign Policy of Modern Japan*. University of California, Berkeley. 1977. pp. 367-390.
2 E. H. Norman, *Origins of the Modern Japanese State*. Pantheon, New York. 1975.
3 Gerrit W. Gong, *The Standard of 'Civilization' in International Society*. Clarendon Press, Oxford. 1984.
4 His armies invaded in 1592, but became bogged down due to guerrillas and Chinese aid to the Koreans. Also, the Japanese navy was defeated by the famous Korean admiral Yi Sunsin, and the invasion force could not be supplied. The forces were withdrawn, and a second invasion attempt failed in 1597. Takakshi Hatada, *A History of Korea*. ABC Clio, Santa Barbara. 1969.
5 Kazuo Kawai, *Japan's American Interlude*. University of Chicago, Chicago. 1960.
6 George Sansom, *A History of Japan 1615-1867*. Stanford University. 1963.
7 Gilbert Rozman (ed.), *The Modernization of China*. The Free Press, New York. 1981.
8 Chalmers Johnson, *MITI and the Japanese Miracle: The Growth of Industrial Policy, 1925-1975*. Stanford University, Stanford. 1982.
9 Edwin O. Reischauer and John K. Fairbank, *East Asia and the Great Tradition*. Houghton Mifflin, Boston. 1960.
10 Cyril Black *et al.*, *The Modernization of Japan and Russia*. The Free Press, New York. 1975.
11 Tatsuo Kawai, *The Goal of Japanese Expansion*. Hokuseido Press, Tokyo. 1938.
12 H. F. MacNair and D. F. Lach, *Modern Far Eastern International Relations*. D. Van Nostrand, New York. 1950.

13 Meirion and Susie Harries, *Sheathing the Sword: The Demilitarization of Japan*. Hamish Hamilton. 1985.
14 Frank C. Langdon, *Japan's Foreign Policy*. University of British Columbia, Vancouver. 1973.
15 John F. O'Connell, "The Role of the Self-Defense Forces in Japan's Sea Lane Defense," *Journal of Northeast Asian Studies*, 3:3, pp. 59-64.
16 Robert E. Bedeski, *The Fragile Entente. The 1978 Japan-China Peace Treaty in a Global Context*. Westview, Boulder, Colorado. 1983.
17 Dennis and Peggy Warner, *The Tide at Sunrise. A History of the Russo-Japanese War, 1904-1905*. Charterhouse, New York. 1974.
18 Chae-Jin Lee, *Japan Faces China. Political and Economic Relations in the Postwar Era*. Johns Hopkins University. 1976.
19 Japan Ministry of Foreign Affairs, *Diplomatic Bluebook 1986 Edition*. Foreign Press Center, Tokyo. 1986.
20 Defense Agency Japan, *Defense of Japan*. The Japan Times, Tokyo. 1986.

The People's Republic of China: An Independent Foreign Policy of Peace

SHEN SHOUYUAN*
and
HUANG ZHONGQING

ABSTRACT

This article traces the evolution of the foreign policy of the People's Republic of China in a historical perspective, analyses the principal imperatives that have shaped the country's current independent policy of peace, and looks into its underlying rationales. Drawing upon a wealth of primary sources, the essay presents a distinctive Chinese view of the current international scene as well as of the international behaviour of the country, which is opening up to the outside world and restructuring its economy in an all-out drive for development.

1. INDEPENDENCE—THE CORNERSTONE

Historical Roots

IN THE PRESENT-DAY WORLD, with the two superpowers locked in a fierce contention for world domination, China is asserting a distinctively independent role. This emphasis on independence has deep historical roots.

China is now underdeveloped economically and has yet a long way to go before it can become a modernized developed nation. The country, however, boasts of one of the world's most ancient civilizations. China's four major inventions in olden times—the compass, gunpowder, paper making and block printing—contributed much to human progress. The Great Wall, one of the world's marvels, and other monuments are still there today to bear witness to a glorious past and a magnificent cultural heritage. All this has fed a national pride, which was badly hurt in modern times when the country was reduced to a powerless semicolony at the mercy of major world powers through a series of armed interventions beginning with the Opium War of 1840. Only after protracted and arduous struggles culminating in an eight-year war against Japanese aggression in 1937-45 and a civil war fought between the Communist-led popular forces and the US-aided Kuomintang did China stand up again in 1949. The traumatic memories of untold miseries and humiliations

* Faculty of Foreign Affairs College, Beijing, China.

suffered by the nation over a century have led the Chinese people to be all the more jealous of their hard-won independence.

China's assertion of independence in its foreign policy is above all manifest in the fact that China does not attach itself to either superpower and refuses to be either's client. A review of the evolution of the country's relations with the United States and the Soviet Union will help towards a better understanding of its independent foreign policy.

Sino-US Antagonism

In 1949, China was reborn into a world divided into two antagonistic camps. The United States was hostile to the new regime in Beijing and continued to support the Kuomintang authorities in Taiwan which claimed to represent the whole of the Chinese people. In an effort to seek a truly independent and equal status in the international community, the People's Republic set itself an immediate task of eliminating the vestiges of foreign domination in China. The new regime, therefore, did not recognize the foreign organizations or diplomats accepted by the Kuomintang as having any legal position in China, and it cancelled traitorous treaties signed by the Kuomintang government. Although willing to establish diplomatic relations with all countries on the basis of equality, the new regime was in no hurry to seek recognition by the United States or any other power that remained hostile.[1] Under the circumstances, the People's Republic identified itself with the socialist camp and allied itself with the Soviet Union in confrontation with the United States. The outbreak of the Korean War in 1950 confirmed and aggravated Sino-US antagonism, which was to last for over twenty years until normalization in the 1970s.

It is significant to note, however, that even in its relations with the Soviet Union in those days, China upheld "the principle of independence and self-reliance,"[2] which was evident in its persistent efforts to acquire independent industrial and defence capabilities and in its implementation of policies with Chinese characteristics in domestic political, social and economic development.

Sino-Soviet Split

After the 20th Congress of CPSU in 1956, differences began to develop between the Chinese and Soviet communist parties, which were soon to evolve into tensions between the two states. In 1958, Moscow's proposal for a joint navy with the People's Republic was turned down by the Chinese government as an attempt at military domination. In July 1960, Moscow withdrew all Soviet experts working in China, thus terminating hundreds of ongoing aid projects. Sino-Soviet economic and trade ties dwindled rapidly thereafter. Moreover, Beijing took alarm at an incipient détente between the Soviet Union and the United States symbolized by the Moscow partial test ban treaty of 1963, which China rejected as a superpower attempt at nuclear monopoly and a denial of its legitimate right to develop independent nuclear capabilities.

The outbreak of bloody border clashes in 1969 brought Sino-Soviet antagonism to a dangerous point until agreement to resume boundary talks was reached at a brief meeting between the Chinese and Soviet premiers at Beijing airport on September 11, 1969. Tension persisted, however, with a massive Soviet military presence on the Chinese border and in Mongolia. In addition, the Soviet backing of Vietnam in occupying Cambodia in 1979 and the Soviet invasion of Afghanistan on China's west in the same year further augmented Moscow's menace to the security of the People's Republic. These constitute what China terms "the three obstacles" to the normalization of Sino-Soviet relations. Under the circumstances, China could hardly be insensitive to the many signs that the Soviet Union was mounting a global strategic offensive. Hence its perception that Moscow constituted "the most dangerous source of war."[3]

Normalization with the US

In the meantime, China and the United States began to normalize their relations after more than twenty years of enmity. US President Richard Nixon's China visit and the resultant Shanghai Communique in 1972 opened a new chapter in bilateral relations. In 1979 formal diplomatic ties were established.

Friendly relations and cooperation between the two countries have witnessed considerable progress since then. Exchange of visits and discussions between officials of the two countries at various levels have furthered mutual understanding. Economic and trade relations, scientific and technical cooperation, educational and cultural exchanges, and contacts between their armed forces have all expanded. Two-way trade grew from US$2.45 billion in 1979 to US$7.3 billion in 1986, making the United States China's third most important trading partner after Japan and Hong Kong. In terms of direct foreign investments in China, the United States takes the first place. By 1986, projects undertaken with direct US investments in China numbered 304, with the total capital contracted exceeding US$2.7 billion, accounting for 13.5% of the total foreign investments in China.[4]

The Taiwan question, nevertheless, has been a source of twists and turns in Sino-American relations and remains a major obstacle to further growth. Shortly after the establishment of diplomatic relations in 1979, a "Taiwan Relations Act" was adopted by the US Congress, which treats Taiwan as an independent political entity. Continued US arms sales to Taiwan, in particular, gave rise to much Chinese resentment. Relations cooled down until the issuance of the 1982 Sino-US joint communique in which the United States undertook to phase out arms sales to Taiwan. Following a process of mutual readjustments, Sino-American relations gradually became stable again. Over the past year, however, China has complained of attacks from the US Congress and other circles on a number of its domestic issues including Tibet.

Obstacles Remain in Sino-Soviet Relations

In recent years, Sino-Soviet relations have improved in some fields. Economic, scientific, technical and cultural exchanges have registered marked growth. The volume of trade, involved in agreements signed by the two countries in 1986, amounted to US$2.6 billion, an increase of 30 per cent over that of 1985. Also, ten rounds of consultations have been held between vice-foreign ministers of the two countries with a view to normalizing bilateral relations. In early 1987, boundary talks were again resumed. Nevertheless, so far no substantial progress has been made in improving political relations as "the three obstacles" are still present.

The question of Cambodia is seen by China as the biggest obstacle in Sino-Soviet relations. In an interview on September 2, 1986, Deng Xiaoping called upon the Soviet Union to urge Vietnam to withdraw its troops from Cambodia, a "hot spot" where "China and the Soviet Union are actually in a state of confrontation", "which takes the form of pitting Vietnamese armed forces against China". While expressing "cautious welcome" to recent overtures from the Soviet Union, Deng stressed that China has to "wait and see" if the latter takes a solid step towards the removal of obstacles to normalized political relations.[5] He pointed out recently that the Soviet Union has *not* changed its position of supporting Vietnam in occupying Cambodia.[6]

What is more, it has been repeatedly stressed by Chinese leaders that even if Sino-Soviet political relations have been normalized, there will be no return to the Sino-Soviet Alliance of the 1950s.[7]

No alliance with Superpowers

It can be seen from the above that at different periods following the founding of the People's Republic, China had to resist pressure from one superpower or the other to safeguard its state sovereignty and independence. It has refused to submit to pressure from either superpower throughout. Deng Xiaoping noted pointedly in his opening speech at the 12th National Congress of the Chinese Communist Party in 1982, "Independence and self-reliance have always been and will forever be our basic stand. We Chinese people value our friendship and cooperation with other countries and people. We value even more our hard-won independence and sovereign rights. No foreign country can expect China to be its vassal or expect it to swallow any bitter fruit detrimental to its own interests."

Drawing on its past experiences, China has made it clear that it will never ally itself or establish strategic relationships with any major power. Premier Zhao Ziyang recently stated, "Maintaining independence, China will not enter into alliance with the superpowers."[8]

2. SAFEGUARDING WORLD PEACE—THE PRIMARY OBJECTIVE OF CHINA'S FOREIGN POLICY

Peace and Development

China's current drive for economic development calls for a peaceful foreign policy. An economically poor and backward country, China can achieve prosperity only through development in peace. The country is now engaged in a long-term modernization programme that requires the sustained efforts of several generations. It needs peace not only in this century, but also in the next. The "fundamental aim" of China's foreign policy, as Foreign Minister Wu Xueqian stated, "is to preserve world peace and secure an enduring peaceful international environment for its socialist modernization."[9]

With top priority given to economic development, China is allocating only an appropriate measure of resources for the maintenance of a necessary defence capacity.[10] Committed to an open policy in the interest of its development programme, the country is expanding its foreign trade and economic co-operation with other countries, and is increasing the inflow of capital, machinery, technology and managerial expertise. All this would be inconceivable in a hostile and unstable international environment.

To have peace and development, China seeks to establish and expand friendly relations with all countries of the world on the basis of the Five Principles of Peaceful Coexistence.[11] It is in favour of a peaceful settlement of international disputes, which has been borne out by the agreements on Hong Kong and Macao's return to China achieved through peaceful negotiations. Furthermore, China has also consistently sought to settle the question of Taiwan's reunification with the mainland by peaceful means under the "one nation, two systems" formula, although the matter comes within China's internal affairs. However, as Deng Xiaoping pointed out, China cannot undertake never to resort to force in settling the Taiwan question because such an undertaking would make peaceful negotiations impossible.[12]

Oppose Hegemonism and Defend World Peace

China is of the view that world peace and national security are closely interrelated. Encroaching upon a nation's independence and sovereignty will undoubtedly jeopardize world peace. It is, therefore, essential to oppose any form of interference in other countries' internal affairs and any form of violation of other countries' sovereignty and territorial integrity, and to oppose in particular any armed aggression against other countries. In other words, in order to preserve world peace, it is necessary to oppose power politics and hegemonism,[13] and particularly to oppose the hegemonist policies pursued by the two superpowers. In the world today, as China sees it, only the United States and the Soviet Union are capable of waging a new world war. The rivalry between the two superpowers for global hegemony is the root cause of most international tensions and the principal threat to global peace.

However, this does not mean that China wants tension in its relations with the superpowers. "We [China] take a principled stand in handling our relations with the United States and the Soviet Union. We will not refrain from improving relations with them because we oppose their hegemonism, nor will we give up our anti-hegemonist stand because we want to improve relations with them," stated Premier Zhao Ziyang in explaining the unique and subtle realism of China's policy towards superpower hegemonism.[14]

China's Position on Arms Race and Disarmament

A principal area of superpower contention is their arms race, which poses a major threat to world peace. China opposes the arms race and the expansion of this race to outer space. It stands for a total ban and destruction of all nuclear, chemical and biological weapons as well as a drastic reduction in conventional arms. The two superpowers have a "special responsibility" for the arms race and therefore disarmament. They are called on to "take the lead" in drastically reducing their nuclear and conventional arsenals. China also maintains that countries, big or small, should have a say on disarmament, that bilateral and multilateral efforts for disarmament should complement and promote each other, that any disarmament talks and agreements between the United States and the Soviet Union should not harm the interests of other countries.[15]

There seems to be a possibility now for the two superpowers to reach some temporary partial arms control agreements. China believes that this is no easy matter and will involve a process of tough bargaining.[16] Still it hopes "the United States and the Soviet Union will continue their dialogues, because, after all, dialogue is better than confrontation."[17] China favours an easing of the tension between the two superpowers, for "when their relations become strained, the danger of war escalates."[18]

As a nuclear state, China strives to make its due contribution to world disarmament. As early as in 1964, China declared explicitly on the very first day when it came into possession of nuclear weapons that at no time and under no circumstances would it be the first to use them. China has also undertaken not to use or threaten to use nuclear weapons against non-nuclear states or nuclear-free zones. China has signed the relevant protocols to the Treaty for the Prohibition of Nuclear Weapons in Latin America and the South Pacific Nuclear Free Zone Treaty. Also, China stands for the principle of non-proliferation of nuclear weapons. Its nuclear cooperation with other countries is confined to the peaceful use of nuclear energy.

In recent years, China has played a more dynamic role in world disarmament efforts. At the 41st session of the United Nations General Assembly in 1986, two draft resolutions which were submitted by the Chinese delegation on nuclear and conventional disarmament were adopted by an overwhelming majority. Meanwhile, China has taken a number of concrete steps in arms reduction. It has cut its armed force by one million servicemen since 1985 and reduced the percentage of its military spending in the state budget from 17.5 per cent in 1979 to 8.28 per cent in 1987. China's total military spending in 1986 was less than US$5.5 billion, accounting for only 0.5% of the world's total.[19] In March 1986, it declared that it would conduct no more atmospheric nuclear tests. A considerable portion of China's military industry has been shifted to civilian production. Some military airports and naval ports have been turned to civilian purposes.

China's position on regional conflicts

Although no new world war has broken out, regional wars have been on and off in the past four decades. Efforts for political settlements of regional issues have proved by and large fruitless, leaving a number of "hot spots" in the world. China does not believe that disarmament alone is enough to safeguard peace. "Peace is indivisible. Tension or conflicts in any region will inevitably affect the peace and stability of the world as a whole," said Foreign Minister Wu Xueqian.[20] "At the same time as efforts are made for disarmament, 'hot spots' in the world should be eliminated."[21]

With regard to regional conflicts, China criticizes the responsible parties, no matter who they may be. "We base our attitude on the merits of each individual case," said Vice-Foreign Minister Qian Qichen. "In our view, whether a particular move or policy in a region is right or wrong cannot simply be determined by judging which social system and ideology the responsible party adheres to, but by judging if the action helps to ease international tension, maintain world peace and promote common prosperity. We oppose any nation, no matter what its politics, that interferes in other nations' internal affairs under whatever pretext, or sends troops to invade other countries, wages a prolonged war there and suppresses the resistance by weak nations," he added.[22] China thus criticizes the Soviet Union for its behaviour in Indochina and Afghanistan, and also disapproves of US intervention in Central America and the Middle East.

Changes in China's Perception of War and Peace

In recent years, Chinese leaders have more than once indicated that China has changed its view that war is inevitable.[23] "Although the present international situation is very complicated and the factor of war still exists, the forces of peace have been growing, and through the joint efforts of the world's people it is entirely possible to attain world peace," stated Premier Zhao Ziyang.[24] China's peaceful foreign policy is thus not only dictated by a compelling need, but is also based on perceived chances for peace in the present-day world.

Deng Xiaoping and other senior Chinese officials have on several occasions expressed hope for peace not only in this century, but also in the next. Indeed, it seems to be a widely-accepted observation among Chinese analysts that a world war seems unlikely by the turn of the century.[25] This optimism is said to be based on "long-term studies and sober analyses of the postwar strategic conditions."[26] Changes on the world scene in favour of the prevention of a new global war have been observed in Chinese analyses:

(1) *A trend towards multipolarity*. Foreign Minister Wu Xueqian referred to "the trend towards multipolarity in international relations" as "a positive factor making for peace," pointing out in this connection the growing role of the newly-independent countries, the numerous non-aligned and other small and medium-sized countries in international affairs.[27] With postwar bipolarity decaying, such major issues as that of war and peace are no longer to be determined by the two superpowers alone, an army paper analysis observed. Most countries, especially the third world nations, are opposed to power politics and military alliance, and are striving for peace and development. Though not in a position to wage a world war, they have the means to boycott and affect any such attempt.[28] Furthermore, "As long as countries in Europe, including Eastern Europe, Oceania, and even Japan do not get tied up in the 'war train', there is much hope of peace," Deng Xiaoping observed.[29] "Whoever launches a war would not win support, even from his allies."[30] In this connection, special importance seems to be attached to Europe.[31] It was recently referred to by Deng as an "area of crucial importance in deciding the question of war or peace."[32]

(2) *The evolution of military technology and the emergence of a strategic balance between the two superpowers*.[33] "Being aware of the enormous destructive power of nuclear weapons, both superpowers have refrained from taking the risk of a nuclear exchange," noted an article in *International Studies*, a journal published by a government-affiliated research institute.[34] An army paper analysis pointed out further, "The evolution of military technology has changed traditional rules of war as well as military thinking, and have produced important effects on the global strategic pattern. In a major nuclear war, both belligerents run great risks of mutual destruction. The greater nuclear capability a nation acquires, the less bold it tends to become to go to war."[35]

Chinese analysts generally seem to believe that overall the United States and the Soviet Union are locked in a strategic stalemate which neither can break in the near future. Characterized by confrontation plus dialogue, current US-Soviet relations will be alternatively strained and relaxed at different periods. Neither superpower is likely to give up contention in times of relaxation, or let any tension in their mutual relations escalate into war.[36]

However, Chinese analyses do not seem to ignore the danger of a world war, that "still exists and will not disappear by itself."[37] As regional conflicts, generally set against a background of superpower rivalry, will not cease to take place, the possibility of such conflicts escalating into a global war cannot be ruled out altogether. Also, if either superpower should acquire an assuredly effective strategic defence system thus breaking the current "balance of terror", the danger of war would drastically increase.[38] China is, therefore, opposed to the extension of the arms race into outer space, which represents a "qualitative escalation" of that race and poses the danger that the race could "go completely out of control," thereby making war more likely.[39]

It may be appropriate to conclude this section with a brief summary of the highlights of a recent interview given by Minister of Defence Zhang Aiping, which throws light on China's current official position on war and peace as well as its strategic thinking. The minister said that in view of the changes on the international scene, *inter alia* the strategic balance between the two superpowers and the growing strength of the peace-loving people and countries against war, China's guideline on national defence has changed greatly over the past two years. In China's view, while there still exists the danger of a world war, the global situation is and will be characterized by relative peace at present and for a considerable period of time to come. According to the minister, China's defence used to be based on preparedness against an early major war, and a nuclear one for that matter. But it is now switching over to a systematic and progressive defence modernization prgoramme with emphasis on priority areas. On the basis of the growth of the national economy, he noted, steady efforts are to be made to step up the modernization of China's armed forces and national defence.[40]

3. THE OPEN POLICY TO PERSIST

After a decade of literal isolation during the disastrous "Cultural Revolution" (1966-76), China initiated a new open policy at the end of 1978.[41] Since then, with China's economy expanding, ties between China and the outside world have grown ever closer. In seven short years, China's foreign trade shot up from US$29.3 billion to US$73.8 billion in 1986.[42] More importantly, the range of China's economic ties has expanded to include not only increased trade with the West but extensive ties with the Third World and revived relations with the nations of the East. Various forms of exchanges, including technical cooperation, joint ventures and construction contracts, have expanded.

To speed up its modernization programme, China is trying its best to absorb foreign investment and technology. Four special economic zones have been set up in Guangdong and Fujian provinces, where the local authorities have been granted extensive administrative powers and overseas investors receive preferential treatment. In addition, the metropolis of Shanghai, 13 other coastal cities and the South China island of Hainan have been given "open" status. Economic legislation is being speeded up to ensure the smooth operation of joint ventures as well as of foreign firms in China. By 1986, a total of 7,775 joint ventures, coöperative enterprises or wholly foreign-owned firms had been approved.[43] From 1979 to 1986, China signed diversified loan agreements covering an aggregate total sum of US$28.9 billion, of which US$20.7 billion has been actually used. By the end of 1986, 116 foreign banks, securities companies or insurance companies from 24 different countries had set up 202 permanent offices in China.[44]

Following Party General Secretary Hu Yaobang's resignation in the wake of student unrest in some major cities, there was speculation that China might close its doors again. But facts have belied this suspicion. While sticking to the socialist road, China is pushing on with domestic reforms which are giving an added impetus to an expansion of all forms of external economic cooperation. During the first six months of 1987, an additional 461 joint ventures, 264 co-operative enterprises and 13 wholly foreign-owned firms were approved, bringing the total number of foreign-invested enterprises to 8,516. The total amount of foreign investments contracted thus reached US$17.176 billion. Of these, the number of joint ventures approved in the six months was 157 more than in the corresponding period of the year before.[45] During the first seven months of 1987, China's total exports exceeded US$20 billion, an increase of 35.3% over that of the corresponding period of the preceeding year.[46] Obviously, the open policy is going to persist as part and parcel of the modernization programme that has produced marked results in boosting production, raising the people's living standard[47] and winning deep-rooted popular support. The keynote of the forthcoming Thirteenth National Congress of the Chinese Communist Party will be the furtherance of reforms and open policy, disclosed Premier Zhao Ziyang recently.[48]

However, pursuance of economic reforms and open policy does not mean any diversion from the socialist orientation. Nor is China boosting foreign economic relations at the expense of political principles. A case in point is China's relations with Japan. Sino-Japanese relations have grown rapidly in many fields since the resumption of diplomatic relations. Particularly marked has been the growth of their economic and trade exchanges. The two countries have been major trading partners in the past few years. Yet, recently, after accepting an appeal from the Taiwan authorities filed in the name of "the Republic of China", the Osaka court in Japan made a ruling to turn over China's state property, the Kokario dormitory used by Chinese students in Kyodo, to the Taiwan authorities. The ruling, denounced by China as an open attempt to create "two Chinas", has cast a shadow on Sino-Japanese relations. China has also been concerned over attempts to build up Japanese military forces beyond purely defensive needs, as well as other signs of a tendency to turn Japan into a major military power and revive militarism.

4. THE DIFFERENTIATION OF THE THREE WORLDS AND CHINA'S IDENTIFICATION WITH THE THIRD WORLD

In 1974, Mao Zedong put forward his theory of the three worlds. According to this theory, as a result of changes in international relations, the world today actually consists of three parts, or three worlds, that are both interconnected and in contradiction to one another. The two superpowers—the United States and the Soviet Union—make up the first world. The developing countries in Asia, Africa, Latin America and other regions make up the third world. The developed countries between the two make up the second world.

The superpowers are locked in a rivalry for world domination. They are the source of a new world war. The countries and people of the third world constitute the main force combating imperialism, colonialism and hegemonism. The second world is a force that can be united with in the struggle against superpower hegemonism. China is a developing socialist country belonging to the third world.[49]

Despite China's changed perception of specific realities, the differentiation of the three worlds seems to remain an underlying rationale of China's foreign policy and analyses. China attaches special importance to identifying itself with the third world, declaring it to be its "basic foreign policy to strengthen its unity and cooperation with the other third world nations".[50]

The third world countries possess three-fourths of the world's population. In China's view, "The emergence and growth of the third world is a major event in contemporary world history, and its influence on the international situation is growing. The third world nations are not only the main force for the prevention of war and the maintenance of peace, but also an indispensable factor in the struggle for the development and common prosperity of the world."[51]

China supports the third world countries in their struggle for maintaining national independence and against foreign aggression and interference. It urges foreign troops to withdraw from Cambodia and Afghanistan, works for a just and reasonable solution to the Middle East question, and supports the struggle of the people in southern African countries and the struggle of Latin American countries against outside interference. With regard to conflicts between third world countries, China has always stood for their solution through negotiation on the basis of equality among parties concerned, and not through arms or threat of arms.[52]

China also backs efforts to strengthen solidarity and cooperation among third world nations and works together with them for mutual development through economic cooperation and aid. It supports the reasonable proposals of Latin American countries to improve the terms of debt repayment, with creditor and debtor nations sharing responsibility and seeking new ways to solve the debt problem. China supports the efforts by OPEC to keep oil prices stable.[53]

While advocating promotion of South-South cooperation, China stresses the great importance of improving North-South relations. It has realistically pointed out that, as the developing countries are still fettered and harmed by the inequitable international economic relations, it would be difficult for them to achieve economic development smoothly through their own efforts only. In recent years, many developing countries have had greater difficulties as a result of falling prices for their major products and trade protectionism. In the interest of the common growth of the world economy, China calls on the developed countries and the entire international community to take practical measures in trade, finance, development and other international economic fields to facilitate the flow of capital and transfer of technology to the developing countries, further increase their access to markets and reduce their debt burden.[54]

It might be interesting to note in this connection that senior Chinese leader Deng Xiaoping boils the present-day international situation down to an "East-West, South-North" issue. According to Chinese Vice-Foreign Minister Qian Qichen's interpretation, in essence it means "the world faces two fundamental problems that concern the future of the human race—peace and development." East-West relationship is an issue of peace, while North-South relationship involves principally, but not merely, an issue of development. "From a long-term point of view, a peaceful and stable world cannot be built with just a few nations enjoying an abundance of wealth while the majority live in poverty."[55]

5. THE FIVE PRINCIPLES OF PEACEFUL COEXISTENCE

In addition to the theory of the differentiation of the three worlds and other rationales underlying Chinese foreign policy that have been discussed above, it seems appropriate to do justice here to the Five Principles of Peaceful Coexistence which China has upheld ever since its early days.

The Five Principles of Peaceful Coexistence—mutual respect for sovereignty and territorial integrity, mutual non-aggression, non-interference in each other's internal affairs, equality and mutual benefit, and peaceful coexistence—were initiated in 1954 by China together with India. These principles are laid down in China's constitution as an essential component of its foreign policy. They have been confirmed in numerous treaties, agreements, joint communiques signed by China and other countries as guiding principles for bilateral relations. Over the years, China has established and developed friendly relations and co-operation with countries throughout the world on the basis of these principles.

The concepts of state sovereignty, equality and non-interference in each other's internal affairs as contained in the Five Principles can be traced back to John Bodin, Hugo Grotius, Thomas Hobbes, Jean Jacques Rousseau and other classical writers of Western political thought between the 16th and 18th centuries, as well as to Emperors Kangxi (1662-1722) and Yongzheng (1723-1735) of China's Qing Dynasty.[56]

When the idea of peaceful coexistence was first advanced by Lenin shortly after the October Revolution of 1917, it was meant to be a principle governing relations between countries of different social systems, namely between the socialist Soviet Union and the capitalist countries. As early as 1956, however, China made it clear that the Five Principles of Peaceful Coexistence should, in its view, serve as the basis for relations between all countries, including those between socialist countries.[57] This has remained China's consistent position.

Based on its own experiences, China seems to be giving new dimensions to these principles by emphasizing their vitality as the basis of relations between states. Premier Zhao Ziyang observed, "Facts of the past 30 years have proved that if countries with different ideologies and social systems follow the Five Principles of Peaceful Coexistence, good relations of mutual confidence will be established between them, and if the Five Principles are violated, such as violating another country's integrity and sovereignty, interference with other countries' internal affairs to benefit oneself at the expense of others, acute confrontation and even conflict may occur between countries with the same ideologies and social systems."[58] "Learning from experiences since the end of World War II," he commented further on another occasion, "we will not let the state of our relationship with other countries be predetermined by the fact whether our social systems and ideologies are similar or not. State relations of different types have emerged since the end of war, but those based on the Five Principles of Peaceful Coexistence have a strong vitality and are most conducive to stability and healthy development of the international situations."[59]

6. REALISM—SEEKING TRUTH FROM FACTS

It can be seen from the above that realism, or emphasis on "seeking truth from facts" as senior Chinese leader Deng Xiaoping puts it, underlies China's foreign policy and analyses of current international trends. Little wonder that in response to the comment that "it seemed that Chinese relations with Capitalist America are better than Chinese relations with the Soviet Communists", Deng Xiaoping pointed out, "China does not regard social systems as a criterion in its approach to problems. The state of relations between China and the United States is determined in the context of their specific conditions, and so is that between China and the Soviet Union."[60]

Realism has also featured current efforts to develop theories of international relations in China. While stressing adherence to Marxist historical materialism and dialectical materialism, China has been drawing upon findings and approaches that have proved valid in Western theoretical studies of international relations. At a forum in Beijing at the end of 1986, Huan Xiang, Director-general of the Centre of International Studies of the State Council of China, indicated a need to draw upon Western international theories. The theories of balance, equilibrium, for instance, he said, should be carefully studied in conjunction with the actual pattern of current international relations, so that it will be possible to effect better analyses of such questions as the triangular relationship between the United States, the Soviet Union and China, and the complicated, protracted, often stalemated struggle between the two superpowers over nuclear disarmament. Also, he believed the defining of our era as "the era of imperialism and proletarian revolution" and class struggle as "the exclusive motive force in the evolution of international relations" might be open to rethinking.[61]

EPILOGUE

This is a Chinese presentation of China's foreign policy. Much has been written by Western scholars in English on the subject. With its indigenous features, a distinctive Chinese version may be of interest to English-speaking readers. That, presumably, is the editor's very purpose in asking our contribution of a Chinese element to the present project. Accordingly, in preparing this essay, we have chosen to draw principally upon Chinese sources for facts and views in an effort to produce a first-hand review of Chinese foreign policy and its determinants. The coauthors alone are responsible for what is said in this essay which does not represent the view of any institution.

NOTES

1 See Mao Zedong, "Report to the Second Plenary Session of Seventh Central Committee of the Communist Party of China", VII., *Selected Works of Mao Zedonq*, Peking: Foreign Languages Press, 1961, Vol. 4, pp. 370-371.

2 See Zhou Enlai, "Report on Problems Concerning the Peace Talks", April 1949, *Selected Works of Zhou Enlai*, Beijing: the People's Publishing House, Vol. I, p. 321.

3 See Chinese Foreign Minister Huang Hua's speech at the U.N. General Assembly, September 29, 1977, *Peking Review*, known now in English as *Beijing Review*, No. 41, October 7, 1977, p. 35.

4 These figures were released by State Councillor Zhang Jingfu at the Sino-US Symposium on Trade and Investment Laws in Beijing on August 18, 1987. See *People's Daily*, August 18, 1987, p. 1.

5 *Beijing Review*, No. 38, September 22, 1986, pp. 4-5. In this interview with Mike Wallace from Columbia Broadcasting System of the United States Deng Xiaoping said that if the question of the Vietnamese invasion of Cambodia is resolved, he will be ready to "go to any place in the Soviet Union to meet with Gorbachev". Recently, however, he remarked that Gorbachev had actually turned down his offer by rejecting any precondition for such a meeting. Deng pointed out that there is a prerequisite, namely, the Soviet Union should urge Vietnam to withdraw its troops from Cambodia. (See report on Deng Xiaoping's conversation with Japanese visitors, *People's Daily*, December 5, 1987, p. 1).

6 Deng indicated this at a meeting with visiting Thai Foreign Minister Siddhi Savetsila on August 25. See *People's Daily*, August 26, 1987, p. 1. Amidst sweet noises coming out of Moscow, Chinese officials have continued to point to the three obstacles in Sino-Soviet relations. (See comments by Chinese Foreign Ministry spokesman, *People's Daily*, January 21, 1988, p. 1, and Acting Chinese Premier Li Peng's conversation with visiting Pakistani Foreign Minister Zain Noorani, *People's Daily*, February 23, 1988, p. 1). In his comments on January 20, 1988, a Chinese Foreign Ministry spokesman said that the Soviet Union has so far failed to take any solid step to urge Vietnam to withdraw its troops from Cambodia though, he noted, it has agreed to discuss the Cambodian question in Sino-Soviet consultations. (*People's Daily*, January 21, 1988, p. 1).

7 Li Xiannian, President of the People's Republic of China, for one, said this in an interview with US reporters during his 1985 visit to the United States. See *Beijing Review*, No. 31, August 5, 1985, p. 14.

8 Zhao Ziyang, "Report on the Work of the Government", delivered at the 5th Session of the 6th National People's Congress on March 25, 1987, *Beijing Review*, No. 16, April 20, 1987, centrefold, p. XX.

9 Wu Xueqian, Speech at the 41st Session of the United Nations General Assembly, *Beijing Review*, No. 40, October 6, 1986, p. 18.

10 Qian Qichen, Speech at the United Nations International Conference on Disarmament and Development, August 25, 1987, *People's Daily*, August 27, 1987, p. 6. Also see

"Minister of Defence Zhang Aiping on the Relationship between National Defence and Economic Development", *World Economic Herald*, No. 350, July 27, 1987, p. 2.

11 These principles will be discussed at length in Part 5.

12 See *Outlook*, No. 37, September 16, 1985, p. 11. Apparently, the implication of this statement is that some quarters in Taiwan might take advantage of such an undertaking to resist any attempt at peaceful reunification.

13 See "Qian Qichen on Peace and Disarmament", *World Affairs*, No. 8, April 16, 1987, p. 3.

14 Zhao Ziyang, "Report on the Work of the Government", delivered at the 2nd Session of the 6th National People's Congress on May 15, 1984, *Beijing Review*, No. 21, May 21, 1984, p. 19.

15 "Foreign Minister Wu Talks about World Situation", *Beijing Review*, No. 2, January 12, 1987, pp. 14-15. See also Wu Xueqian, *op. cit.*, pp. 14-15.

16 Zhao Ziyang said this in his conversation with visiting Dutch Prime Minister Rudolphus Lubbers on May 11, 1987. See *People's Daily*, May 12, 1987, p. 1.

17 "Foreign Minister Wu Talks about World Situation", *Beijing Review*, No. 2, January 12, 1987, p. 17.

18 "Qian Qichen Reviews China's Foreign Policy", *Beijing Review*, No. 1, January 6, 1986, p. 15.

19 See Qian Qichen, Speech at the United Nations International Conference on Disarmament and Development, cited in *China Daily*, Aug. 27, 1987, p. 4, and in *People's Daily*, Aug. 27, 1987, p. 6. In the state budget for 1987, expenditures for national defence accounted for only 20.376 billion yuan, 8.28% of the total expenditures projected at 245.946 billion yuan. (See Wang Bingqian, State Councillor and Minister of Finance, "Report on the Implementation of the State Budget for 1986 and on the Draft State Budget for 1987", *Beijing Review*, No. 17, April 27, 1987, centrefold, p. VII).

20 Wu Xueqian, *op. cit.*, p. 15.

21 "Foreign Minister Wu Talks about World Situation", *Beijing Review*, No. 2, January 12, 1987, p. 15.

22 "Qian Qichen Reviews China's Foreign Policy", *Beijing Review*, No. 1, January 6, 1986, p. 14.

23 Deng Xiaoping himself reiterated this at a recent meeting with former Japanese Prime Minister Takeo Fukuda. See *China Daily*, April 24, 1986, p. 1.

24 Zhao Ziyang, "Report on the Work of the Government", delivered at the 5th Session of the 6th National People's Congress on March 25, 1987, *loc. cit.*

25 See Huan Xiang, Director-general of the Centre of International Studies of the State Council of China, "Interview with *World Affairs*", *World Affairs*, No. 1, January 1, 1987, pp. 11-13. A summary of the interview appeared in *People's Daily*, January 3, 1987, p. 6. Also see: Peng Di, "The Current Global Strategic Position and Prospects for World Peace", *Jiefangjun Bao* (The Liberation Army Daily), January 2, 1987, p. 3; and "Round-up of a Seminar on US-Soviet Relations and Their Mutual Policy Trends", *World Affairs*, No. 9, April 22, 1987, pp. 2-12.

26 Li Dai and Zhou Yang, "A Concise Analysis of War and Peace in the World Today", *International Studies*, July, 1986 No. 3, pp. 1-5.

27 Wu Xueqian, *op. cit.*, p. 18.

28 Peng Di, *loc. cit.*

29 "Excerpts from Deng Xiaoping's Conversations with Foreign Visitors in May-September 1986", *Outlook*, No. 44, 1986.

30 Deng said this at a meeting with visiting Icelandic Prime Minister Steingrimur Hermannsson on October 28, 1986. See *Beijing Review*, No. 45, November 10, 1986, p. 6.

31 For a full review of Chinese-European relations, see Shen Shouyuan, "Sino-European Relations in the Global Context: Increased Parallels in an Increasingly Plural World", *Asian Survey*, Vol. XXVI, No. 11, November 1986, University of California Press, Berkeley.

32 Deng said this in his recent meeting with visiting Dutch Prime Minister Rudolphus Lubbers on May 12, 1987. See *People's Daily*, May 13, 1987, p. 1.

33 Some sophisticated analyses of the arms race and military balance between the United States and the Soviet Union can be found in the Chinese media. See Shi Wuqing, "Superpowers Reach Military Balance", *Journal of International Studies* (known now as *International Studies*), No. 1, January 1985. An abridged translation of the article appears in *Beijing Review*, Nos. 3&4, January 21&28, 1985.

34 Li Dai and Zhou Yang, *loc. cit. International Studies* is a journal published by the Institute of International Studies, a research institute affiliated with the Ministry of Foreign Affairs.

35 Peng Di, *loc. cit.*

36 See Huan Xiang, *loc. cit.* Also see "Round-up of a Seminar on US-Soviet Relations and Their Mutual Policy Trends", *World Affairs*, No. 9, April 22, 1987, pp. 2-12.

37 Peng Di, *loc. cit.*

38 Peng Di, *loc. cit.* Also see Li Dai and Zhou Yang, *loc. cit.*

39 "Deng Xiaoping's Interview with *Outlook*", *Outlook*, No. 37, September 16, 1985.

40 Minister of Defence Zhang Aiping's interview, *World Economic Herald*, No. 350, July 27, 1987, p. 2.

41 The open policy was officially instituted at the 3rd Session of the 11th Central Committee of the Chinese Communist Party in December 1978.

42 Song Ping, State Councillor and Minister in Charge of the State Planning Commission, "Report on the Draft 1987 Plan for National Economic and Social Development" (Excerpts) delivered at the 5th Session of the 6th National People's Congress on March 26, 1987, *Beijing Review*, No. 17, April 27, 1987, centrefold, p. I.

43 *People's Daily*, May 28, 1987, p. 6.

44 These figures were released by Chen Muhua, Governor of the People's Bank of China, in a speech at the Sino-U.S. Symposium on Trade and Investment Laws in Beijing on August 17, 1987. See *People's Daily*, August 18, p. 4.

45 Statistics by the Chinese Ministry of Foreign Economic Relations and Trade, cited in *People's Daily*, July 25, 1987, p. 1.

46 Statistics by the Chinese Ministry of Foreign Economic Relations and Trade, cited in *People's Daily*, August 15, 1987, p. 1.

47 China's national income in 1986 was 779 billion yuan as compared with 242 billion yuan in 1976. In 1986 total grain output came to 391.09 million tons, cotton 3,540,000 tons, cloth 15,800,000,000 metres, watches 64,450,000, TV sets 14,470,000, tape recorders 16,390,000, cameras 2,150,000, household washing machines 8,990,000, coal 870,000,000 tons, crude oil 131,000,000 tons, output of electricity amounted to 445.5 billion kwh., steel output reached 52.05 million tons, rolled steel 40,540,000 tons. (See: Zhao Ziyang, "Report on the Work of the Government" delivered at the 5th Session of the 6th National People's Congress on March 25, 1987, *Beijing Review*, No. 16, April 20, 1987, centrefold, p. III; "Communique on the Statistics of 1986 Economic and Social Development", *Beijing Review*, No. 9, March 2, 1987, p. 21; and Zhang Zhongji, Director of the Department of Integrated Statistics under the State Statistical Bureau, "End of Turmoil Brings Economic Growth", *Beijing Review*, No. 39, September 29, 1986, p. 18).
According to a source in the Economic Research Centre of the State Planning Commission, from 1978 to 1986, consumption levels of urban and rural population rose from 175 yuan to 452 yuan, registering an average annual increase of 8.1% after allowing for price rises; the per capita housing for rural population increased from 8.1 to 15.3 square metres, that for urban population from 3.6 square metres in 1978 to 6.1 square metres in 1986; from 1978 to 1986, the per capita grain consumption of urban and rural population increased from 195.5 to 256 kilogrammes, an increase of 31%, and the per capita meat consumption from 7.7 to 14.3 kilogrammes, an increase of 85.7%. (*People's Daily*, July 25, 1987, p. 2).

48 Zhao Ziyang disclosed this at a meeting with visiting Foreign Minister Siddhi Savetsila of Thailand. See *People's Daily*, August 21, 1987, p. 1.

49 See (1) Deng Xiaoping's speech at the Special Session of the United Nations Assembly, April 10, 1974; and (2) Editorial Department of the *People's Daily*, "Chairman Mao's Theory of the Differentiation of the Three Worlds Is a Major Contribution to Marxism-Leninism", *People's Daily*, November 1, 1977.

50 "Qian Qichen Reviews China's Foreign Policy", *Beijing Review*, No. 1, January 6, 1986, p. 14.
51 *Ibid.*
52 "Foreign Minister Wu Xueqian Talks About World Situation", *Beijing Review*, No. 2, January 12, 1987, pp. 16-17.
53 *Ibid.*
54 Wu Xueqian, Speech at the 41st Session of the UN General Assembly, *Beijing Review*, No. 40, October 6, 1986, p. 17.
55 "Qian Qichen Reviews China's Foreign Policy", *Beijing Review*, No. 1, January 6, 1986, p. 15.
56 Zhang Zhiyi, "The Historical Perspective of the Grand Idea of Peaceful Coexistence", *Journal of Foreign Affairs College*, No. 2, September 1985, Beijing, pp. 1-2.
57 See "Statement of November 11, 1956 by the Government of the People's Republic of China on the Declaration of October 30, 1956 by the Government of the Soviet Union", *Selected Sources on History of International Relations*, Wuhan University Press, 1983, Vol. II, p. 461.
58 Zhao Ziyang, Speech at the Forum in Beijing to Mark the 30th Anniversary of the Formulation of the Five Principles of Peaceful Coexistence on July 18, 1984, *Beijing Review*, No. 31, July 30, 1984, pp. 16-17.
59 Zhao Ziyang, Speech at the Royal Institute of International Affairs, London, June 6, 1985.
60 Deng Xiaoping said this in an interview with Mike Wallace from Columbia Broadcasting System of the United States on September 2, 1986. See *Beijing Review*, No. 38, September 22, 1986, p. 38.
61 *World Affairs*, No. 1, January 1, 1987, p. 13.

Australian Diplomatic Practice: Methods and Theory

(WITH SPECIAL REFERENCE TO AUSTRALIAN-ASIAN RELATIONS)

RUSSELL B. TROOD*

ABSTRACT

This essay examines aspects of the theory and method behind Australian diplomacy, paying particular attention to the way it has affected relations with Asia. It argues that although Australia took a long period of time to develop an independent posture in international affairs, a distinctive tradition of diplomacy began to emerge much earlier. This evolved within the context of the imperial system and was partly a response to perceived deficiencies in arrangements for dominion representation. Founded on a determinedly Eurocentric outlook towards world affairs and lacking any strong theoretical underpinning, Australia's diplomatic methods, as with its foreign policy in general, have not always been conducive to the development of the closer relations with Asian governments which most postwar Australian governments have desired. Australia's diplomatic performance in Asian has thus been uneven. Australia now devotes more of its modest diplomatic resources to the conduct of its foreign policy in Asian countries than to the maintenance of relations with countries in any other region. While this has enabled Canberra to improve its diplomatic performance in Asia, the economic, political and cultural differences that divide Australia from its neighbours, continue to confront Australian governments with a difficult challenge in the pursuit of their regional diplomatic objectives.

IT HAS BEEN SAID, perhaps with only slight exaggeration, that Australian diplomacy was born at the Paris Peace Conference of 1919.[1] There, in the ostentatious, somewhat unlikely surroundings of Louis XIV's grand palace of Versailles, an Australian prime minister, W. H. (Billy) Hughes, was among several dominion leaders to sit as a member of the British Empire delegation helping to make the post World War I peace of Europe. Amid a congregation that included the most distinguished statesmen of the age, Hughes was to pursue Australia's interests with a single-mindedness that earned him in equal measure both the admiration and the enmity of the select company in which he was moving. The Prime Minister's tactics were impulsive, his policies inflexible, his manner offensive and yet his performance a modest triumph for both the man and the small, relatively inconsequential nation he led. Long before Australians acquired either the capacity or the enthusiasm for an autonomous role in international affairs, Hughes effectively laid the foundations of a diplomatic tradition which endures nearly 70 years later.

* Division of Asian and International Studies, Griffith University, Brisbane, Australia.

This essay seeks to examine aspects of that diplomatic tradition and the assumptions upon which it rests, paying particular attention to Australia's relations with Asia. The discussion is divided into three parts. The first considers the emergence of Australian diplomacy within the context of an evolving foreign policy. Having provided something of an historical background, attention is turned towards the principal institutions, the practitioners and the general style of contemporary Australian diplomacy. The third section discusses the impact of Australian diplomatic methods on relations with the states of South, Southeast and East Asia. The short conclusion discusses the role of theory in the evolution of Australian diplomacy.

Foreign Policy and the Evolution of Australian Diplomacy

When the Commonwealth of Australia was founded in 1901, its political leaders did not seriously consider the possibility of pursuing an independent foreign policy. According to Australia's first prime minister, Edmund Barton, "(t)here could be no foreign policy of the Commonwealth ... foreign policy belong(s) to the Empire,"[2] and for the most part Australians agreed. For several decades they were largely content to define their place in world affairs by reference to their country's status as a dominion within the British Empire rather than as an autonomous independent actor within the wider international system. Isolated from the events and capitals that determined the ebb and flow of world affairs, Australians held opinions about foreign policy but left the conduct of their international affairs to Britain.[3]

Yet within the imperial system Australia had some elementary concerns.[4] Britain could properly claim to represent Empire interests in the international arena, but that did not preclude the need for the Australian and British governments to consult and negotiate over a wide range of issues. Indeed the contrary. If Australia's interests within the imperial system were to be safeguarded, worries over Empire trade, Pacific security and Asian immigration to Australia, for instance, it was imperative that its views be made known to London. Being of direct importance to Australia's security and prosperity, many of these issues were seen to demand the close attention of the prime minister. As a consequence he and his small group of administrative officials became figures of cardinal importance in the making and conduct of Australia's "external" relations. Their active involvement in all aspects of the policy process tended to preclude the development of diplomatic institutions, such as an independent foreign service, but their exposure to the imperatives of "international" affairs nevertheless demanded a measure of diplomatic energy and expertise. Moreover, there were occasions when Australia's early governments resisted the constraints of the imperial system and gained international experience independent of London. In 1901, for instance, the Deakin government negotiated an immigration agreement with Japan, and in 1908, against London's strong objections, Australia invited America's Great White Fleet to pay a goodwill visit.[5] But until the advent of war in Europe in 1914 such events were rare.

With the coming of war, Australia's willing support of British interests demanded, at least from an antipodean perspective, a revision of the mechanisms for Imperial policy making. Earlier attempts at this had yielded very little and for a time the British government continued to resist change. But dominion losses on the battlefield were to make further opposition untenable, and eventually dominion, especially Australian, efforts to make the imperial system more responsive to their interests resulted in the creation of an imperial War Cabinet.[6] After the war Hughes' conviction, shared by other dominion leaders on behalf of their own countries, that Australia's contribution to the Empire war effort entitled it to a part in the peace negotiations resulted in pressure to attend the Paris Conference.[7] Although London acceded and Australia joined the other dominions as part of the British Commonwealth delegation, Hughes participated with a distincly Australian national agenda in mind. His aggressive pursuit of Australian interests over matters such as reparations, New Guinea and racial inequality did not succeed entirely, but in the evolution of Australia diplomacy this is not the salient point. Hughes made a tremendous impact on the conference and by his actions took Australian diplomacy outside the narrow confines of the imperial system and into a much wider international arena. In doing so he established, albeit temporarily, his small country's presence on the international stage.

Yet this was a presence, and Paris laid foundations, upon which neither Hughes nor his immediate successors were pleased to build. After 1919 Australia retreated to a place of near isolation in international affairs. Nearly 20 years later, Richard Casy, Australia's "liaison officer" in London, captured the sentiment of the inter-war years when he remarked that Australians "do not want to bother anybody else and we do not want to be bothered."[8] At a time when other Commonwealth dominions, notably Canada and South Africa, were beginning to show signs of greater independence in the conduct of their foreign relations, Australia shrank from the prospect, believing that displays of dominion independence might threaten "the diplomatic unity of the Empire."[9] A High Commission established in London in 1910 remained Australia's only foreign diplomatic mission and all suggestions for change—to establish diplomatic contact with the Americans, for example—were defeated. In such an environment the institutions of Australian diplomacy also remained in a retarded state of development. It was 1929 before a modest step was taken toward the development of a professional foreign service. After several years of effort by a small group of officials including Dr. Walter Henderson, approval was given for certain officers of the public service to undertake specific duties relating to Australia's external interests. These officials, however, were to remain under administrative authority of the prime minister's department.[10] But after his reform it was another six years before the external affairs function of the prime minister's office was detached and allocated to a separate Department of External Affairs with its own organizational structure, permanent head, specialized staff and minister.[11]

It took the growing prospect of war in Asia and the Pacific to force more wide-ranging reforms. Increasingly uneasy at both the belligerent course of Japanese policy in the Far East and Britain's apparent inability to do anything about it,[12] the Menzies government moved to expand Australia's diplomatic contacts with the more important states of the region, and to take a more active role in local affairs. "What Britain calls the Far East," Menzies told a broadcast audience in April 1939, "is to us the near north. Little given as I am to encouraging exaggerated ideas of Dominion independence I see no reason why we should not play an effective part in the affairs of the Pacific."[13] As Alan Watt points out, the announcement did not amount to a declaration of independence from British foreign policy. Even so, it did signal a break with the past. Australia was not only to expand substantially hitherto limited diplomatic contacts with countries outside the Commonwealth; it was about to develop some independent capacity to gather intelligence and monitor its own foreign interests. To this extent there were signs of Australia moving toward a more autonomous role in international affairs.

With the advent of war this rather belated movement towards greater autonomy rapidly gained momentum. In this process, events in the Asia-Pacific region were crucial. Japan's southerly thrust into the area confronted Australia with "the dire peril of invasion by a ferocious enemy" and the greatest ever threat to its security. When imperial defence arrangements, based on the Singapore strategy, proved inadequate for Australia's defence, Anglo-Australian relations reached an historic nadir and John Curtin's Labour government turned to the United States to help avert the danger.[14] These events had an enduring impact on Australians. The notion, hitherto only dimly understood, that Australia had a set of national interests independent of and separable from these of other countries was forcefully brought home. The folly of allowing another government, even that of a presumed close friend or ally, to assume responsibility for Australia's security had been highlighted. The need for Australia not only to design and implement its own security guarantees, but, more broadly, to discover new foundations for the conduct of its foreign relations had been made compellingly clear. Finally, the prospects of Australia being able to undertake a more active and important role in the international arena had been greatly enhanced by domestic reforms to procedures for policy formulation.

The war was also a catalyst for the growth of Australian diplomacy. External Affairs was not a designated war department and did not, therefore, expand to the same degree as say, defence.[15] But with an energetic minister in the person of Dr. H. V. Evatt and a central role in post-war policy planning, it was able to achieve and consolidate a place of growing prominence among the external affairs departments of the federal bureaucracy. At the same time, the Chifley government's commitment to an activist and generally more independent foreign policy encouraged the rapid growth of the foreign service.

In 1943, Evatt had introduced a scheme for recruiting cadet diplomats, and this served as the basis for selecting new and much-needed junior personnel. Over three years from mid-1946 the Department experienced a threefold increase in staff, while Australia's overseas missions grew over a slightly longer period (1945-49) from nine to twenty-six.[16]

This immediate post-war period was one of exceptional growth for both External Affairs and Australia's diplomatic service. In the 40 years since, the experience has not been repeated. But for much of this time both the department and the service enjoyed steady growth despite periodic changes in government. That this has been so reflects the broad political consensus that has continued to mark post-war Australian foreign policy. While governments have naturally disagreed, sometimes vehemently, over specific issues and policies, all have tended to subscribe to a common set of assumptions about Australia's place in the international system, the nature of its foreign interests and the means to secure those interests. This has provided relatively stable parameters for the conduct of Australian diplomacy. There have been no radical changes in the direction of Australia's foreign policy, and similarly, no sudden, substantial changes in the methods and practices of its diplomacy. Reform of diplomatic processes and structures has generally been incremental leaving, as will now be discussed, elements of Australia's earliest diplomatic practices firmly in place.

The Character of Australian Diplomacy

Institutions and Practitioners. At federation the forms and processes of British diplomacy offered a model for Australians to emulate. In a country as thoroughly British in outlook, culture and political tradition as Australia then was, and whose external policy was Anglo-centric, this was natural; indeed, it could hardly have been otherwise. Nevertheless, it took relatively little time for Australia's political leaders to appreciate that the demands of making and conducting external policy in and for a remote dominion were different to those for a great imperial power. British diplomatic methods, it was thus reasoned, could have only limited application in Australia. The new federation had to create many of its own diplomatic processes, particularly in establishing institutions and deciding how they should relate to one another. In Australia, for example, the considerable authority enjoyed by the Foreign Office in the conduct of British foreign policy, was not replicated, nor did foreign ministers enjoy comparative preeminence. It is an overlooked point in the history of Australian diplomacy that during the period prior to the Second World War when Australia contentedly accepted Britain's conduct of its foreign relations, the elements of a distinctively Australian diplomatic tradition were already clearly emerging.[17]

It is useful to begin by establishing context.[18] Australia is a federation with governmental responsibilities divided primarily between two levels of state and federal government. The latter has constitutional authority over external affairs, but the states have always had a modest role in the area. Of late they have began to intrude more actively into this area and successive federal administrations have often deemed it in their political interests to accommodate to pressures rather than invoke strict constitutional fiat.[19] Yet it is essentially correct to say that in Australia, as in other federations, foreign policy is a federal function, and as in other parliamentary systems it is the preserve of the political executive. The prime minister and his colleagues in Cabinet set policy objectives, establish their priority, allocate resources to their pursuit and monitor progress towards their attainment. On pain of foreign policy failure, perhaps disaster, these tasks cannot but be successfully performed.

Yet Cabinet's exclusive burden is largely a constitutional one. Practically, the formulation and implementation of policy are activities undertaken in conjunction with other elements of government, meaning, when disaggregated, specific institutions and particular individuals. Within a Cabinet system, ministers and the departments for which they are responsible are of abiding importance. In the foreign policy arena within Australia, the roles of prime minister and their respective departments of state are central. Their separate and co-ordinated performances in policy formulation and implementation determine above all others within government, the quality of the nation's foreign policy. It is from among this relatively small group of key actors that one finds the essential institutions and practitioners of Australia diplomacy.

The Department of Foreign Affairs and Trade[20] has a natural claim to being regarded as the pre-eminent bureaucratic institution of Australian foreign policy. That this is no more than a claim reflects the reality that its singular status has never been entirely secure. From the time of its original creation as External Affairs in 1901, the department has enjoyed mixed fortunes, frequently being forced to fight for bureaucratic turf against the claims of other departments. So weak was its position during the first decades after federation that in 1916 it virtually disappeared from the bureaucratic landscape, to be absorbed within the prime minister's department.[21] Even since its reincarnation as a separate department in 1935, the challenges to its authority have persisted.[22]

Legacies of weakness aside, however, the contemporary problem confronting Foreign Affairs, and therefore Australian diplomacy in general, is the large number of federal departments of state possessing, or claiming to possess, policy functions touching Australia's foreign interests. In addition to foreign affairs, departments with mandates in areas of defence, trade, primary industry, education, immigration and finance, not to mention several national security agencies, are among the most prominent. In addition the prime minister's department has responsibilities touching all these areas. That the functions of these departments may overlap and that issues may result in the interests of different agencies becoming intertwined is a hazard of modern government and not, of course, unique to Australia. In Canberra as elsewhere, mechanisms such as inter-departmental committees exist to curtail the bureaucratic fallout from these difficulties. Where they lead to conflict, as Foreign Affairs' own experience testifies, it may be bureaucratic gamesmanship and not the merit of a position that wins out. For reasons related to the nature of its responsibilities, its distinctive departmental culture and its marginal role within the public service bureaucracy, Foreign Affairs has often lacked the skills to compete in this environment. But the point of particular importance here is that in the foreign policy arena, departmental rivalries at home can quickly translate into policy conflicts abroad subverting national priorities and causing incoherence in the conduct of policy. That neither Foreign Affairs nor any other department of state has enjoyed the kind of authority or political support needed to prevent such situations, has been a cost to Australian diplomacy.

Historically, the defence and prime minister's departments have been amongst Foreign Affairs most consistent rivals: the former because it acquired early authority over the issue of empire security which, above all others, was most central to Australia's early relations with Britain, and the latter because therein was vested the locus of external policy making. But in the postwar conduct of Australian diplomacy, Foreign Affairs has also been forced to contend with departments, styled under various nomenclatures, exercising trade functions. In Australia, Departments of Trade existed in one form or another long before the war and were able to build up a considerable amount of experience in the external arena.[23] With the rapid expansion of Australia's international trade after 1945 they were able to consolidate their position and pose a special challenge to Foreign Affairs' status, particularly when the portfolios were held by senior Country party ministers in Menzies' coalition governments during the 1950s and 1960s.

Recent administrative reforms have brought major changes to this area of Australian diplomacy. Of these, the most significant is the Hawke government's July 1987 decision to merge Foreign Affairs with the Department of Trade.[24] The rationale for creating a Department of Foreign Affairs and Trade, as the new agency is called, has never been fully disclosed, but it appears to owe much to the government's conviction about the importance of trade and international economic issues on Australia's contemporary foreign policy agenda.

The full import of the union has yet to emerge, but already some things are clear. Initially there has been administrative disruption and upheaval as two departments of fundamentally different bureaucratic cultures and structures, with a long tradition of rivalry, have attempted to meld their interests and attitudes into a cohensive organization. Foreign service personnel have lost their preferred status in appointment to diplomatic posts abroad and in departmental positions at home. Bureaucratic conflicts of interest between rival departments will, of course, be eliminated, though there are early indications that some of these have emerged within the new organization. The long term outlook, however, should be one of greater coherence in the making and implementation of policy in the trade area and an enhanced effectiveness to diplomacy in important markets such as Japan, the Middle East and among the countries of the European Community. Finally, the merger seems likely to enhance the status of the foreign minister within Cabinet. Lacking an obvious domestic constituency successive ministers have often been aware that despite its prestige, the portfolio has not always given them political leverage in government. By contrast, the trade portfolio has always enjoyed a relatively well-defined and powerful constituency, which will now doubtless be looking to the foreign minister to represent its interests.

The merger with Trade has given impetus to internal changes already underway in Foreign Affairs. These have had the twofold effect of bringing the department into the mainstream of the federal public service and retiring a traditional assumption of foreign office elitism. The latter was partly cultivated by those within Foreign Affairs who rightly saw diplomacy as an especially demanding profession requiring individuals of particular talents and qualities. It was reinforced by the specialized methods of recruiting young foreign service trainees, by the exacting and high standard of selection criteria, by the training and career paths followed by officers once they joined, and by the special privileges attaching to their employment. This elitism was a dimension of what Collins has labelled the "separatist conception" of a foreign office.[25] In Australia, separatism failed to command an acceptance comparable to that enjoyed by the foreign office in London, but, nonetheless, it lent a distinctive character to the Foreign Affairs department and the Australian foreign service. That this is now fading is a reflection of some powerful contemporary pressures: ministerial moves to make the foreign service more open, accessible and accountable; a desire on the part of the Hawke government to introduce comprehensive corporate management techniques throughout the public sector; a reconstitution of the foreign policy issue agenda which now reflects the fusion between socio-economic and politico-security matters; and the declining utility of simple distinctions between foreign and domestic policy issues, a reality that challenges the logic of public service structures in which they are divided for administrative purposes.

While reform of departmental methods is certain to continue, some elements of the Australian diplomatic tradition will probably prove highly resistent to change. Although it was not the conception on which the Australian foreign service or the department was founded, the idea that Australia's professional diplomats should function as both formulators and as implementors of foreign policy has since become central to the whole character of Australian diplomacy. Application of the principle requires that officers be regularly rotated between representative duties abroad and policy and administrative responsibilities at home.[26] In Australia's foreign office, as in many others, the rationale for the fusion of functions has become virtually incontestable: it complements the practice of other states, facilitating intergovernmental communication and cooperation; it allows more efficient use of usually scarce resources; it provides a more satisfying employment structure for professional officers, and perhaps most persuasively, it recognises the essential inseparability of the two functions. As Collins remarks, it is a fundamental requirement of a sound foreign policy that those who offer advice about the world have some experience of and exposure to the forces and pressures that shape it.[27] Conversely, regular home service exposes officers directly to the policy priorities and objectives of the governments they serve.

As the regular complaints of departmental officers testify, Foreign Affairs' efforts to achieve the right mix and balance between foreign and home service for its personnel has long been a source of debate and controversy. Partly this is because the issue is allied to another which is integral to effective foreign policy management, namely the balance between generalism and specialization. Should one be pursued at the expense of the other? Are they mutually exclusive? Foreign Affairs' answer has always been to insist that its officers gain wide-ranging experience in all aspects of the department's responsibilities. Not only have they not been encouraged to develop regional policy specialities (in, for example, Southeast Asia) they have been discouraged from pursuing career paths which preclude some experience of departmental administration and management and of working in functional areas, such as on disarmament or economic policy. While some officers have no doubt been able to avoid such eclectic career experience, for most, diversity and generalism has been the norm.

But the practice has had its critics. Among the most notable has been Gregory Clark, a former foreign service officer who resigned in dissillusionment in 1965. A decade later Clark delivered a broadside against the department in which he criticised, among other things, its commitment to generalism: "What the department wants is generalists ... tag yourself as a narrow specialist and you are finished," he was told in 1961.[28] This attitude, Clark holds, contributed to several policy failures in Asia during the 1960s. From a policy-making perspective there is clearly some advantage in building areas of expertise among departmental officers, particularly in regions of compelling national interest, such as Asia and the Pacific are to Australia. Yet there is no easy way to balance this need against the advantages of officers having broad overall perspectives on the country's international interests, or against their personal career preferences and the need for effective management of limited resources. Clearly Foreign Affairs' efforts to come to terms with the dilemmas posed by these realities have not been particularly successful, but then other foreign offices have faced similar problems. Soon after becoming president, John Kennedy discovered his own State department was unable to suggest reforms that would satisfactorily address the weaknesses engendered by its own commitment to generalism.[29]

Shifting the focus of the discussion away from institutions and more towards the practitioners of Australian diplomacy, it is evident that the problems with which professional foreign service officers have been confronted, as a result of challenges to and reforms within their own department, is part of a much wider assault on their status. The pressures which are animating this assault are not all of recent or contemporary origin. For a long while after federation, a professional foreign service was seen as a dispensable element of foreign policy. The residue of this attitude remains. To be sure Australia's professional diplomats have long been an integral part of Australia's presence abroad, undertaking the tasks of communication, negotiation and representation which are the essence of diplomatic endeavour, but their role has always been heavily undercut by busy amateurs—those whose public duties provide them with either opportunity for or the responsibility to undertake diplomatic activities for which they are not specifically fitted.

Most notable have been Australia's political leaders. Federal Cabinet ministers with departments having overseas interests have long seen it as an indispensable part of their responsibilities to apply their talents to diplomatic tasks, either at home or abroad, when circumstances have dictated. While the portfolios of prime minister and foreign minister naturally attract the heaviest burdens in this regard, the list of Cabinet diplomatists is extensive: ministers of defence, primary industry, immigration, trade and the Treasurer, being among them.

Politics being an uncertain business, the quality of ministerial diplomacy is naturally varied: individuals adopt their own style and this generally reflects personal qualities of education, background and experience. Departments may be able to guide and shape ministerial performances, but ultimately their role is limited by a minister's supreme administrative authority. Ministers frequently accept advice, but they also wilfully decline it, In 1971, for instance, prime minister John Gorton deflected all entreaties that he allow a Foreign Affairs's official to accompany him on a visit to the United States. "They are all the same," he is reported to have said, "Hopeless ... so and so's."[30] Such contempt for official advice, is only one of many reasons that make ministerial ventures in diplomacy something of a hazard for all professional diplomats. Yet, if anything, the trend is for ministerial diplomacy to increase. Partly as a function of growing interdependence and the collapse of the foreign policy agenda into the domestic agenda, political leaders appear to have become convinced that management of the world problems, whether at a bilateral of multilateral level, will be assisted by their timely intervention. In Australia, the frequency with which federal ministers undertake sometimes arduous overseas visits or can be found at home meeting with the representatives of a foreign state testify to the significance of their activities as a facet of the nation's contemporary diplomacy.

Here it is necessary to underscore the special role played by Australia's prime ministers; "Foreign policy," Alfred Deakin remarked to Edmund Barton in 1900, "should always be the preserve of the premier of the day."[31] Thus in the decades immediately after federation, when Australia's external relations consisted primarily of managing relations with London, the prime minister was the most conspicuous practitioner of Australian diplomacy. Since then prime ministerial practice has varied considerably, but overall most Australian premiers have accepted Deakin's 1900 injunction. In part, domestic pressures can be held to account. Few prime ministers are unable to see the possible electoral advantage in diplomatic (adventure), especially when their domestic political stocks may be low. But it is the political and constitutional arangement that permits such a response which is the key to explanation: parliament's relatively inconsequential role in the policy process, the dominance of the political executive, the prime minister's wide authority as head of government, and a largely uncircumscribed discretion to establish the agenda of government all facilitate the prime ministerial role.

With such wide-ranging discretion Australian prime ministers are apt to set their own diplomatic priorities, pursuing them according to personal taste and temperament. Ben Chifley appears to have satisfied his modest interest in foreign policy by offering guidance and leaving much of both the administration and conduct of policy to his enthusiastic foreign minister, Evatt. In contrast, Gough Whitlam, a later Labour prime minister with a much stronger interest in foreign policy, preferred to hold the foreign affairs portfolio unto himself during his government's first 15 months of office, and to undertake numerous personal diplomatic initiatives, both at home and abroad.[32] Nor has it been unusual for Australian prime ministers to reserve either specific issues or special relationships for their personal attention. Anglo-Australian relations remained a particular preserve of prime ministers until the late 1960s, while Australia's relationship with the Peoples Republic of China is one in which successive premiers have maintained a distinctive interest since 1972. At present, prime minister Hawke is taking an active role in Australian efforts to reform aspects of the international trade system. Finally, prime ministerial activism has implications for the management of the foreign policy process. In particular prime ministerial preference can determine the extent of other ministers' policy involvement: harmonious relations between the premier and his colleagues can facilitate the policy process; adversarial relations jeopardise it. In the critical relationship between prime minister and foreign minister Australia's experience has been mixed. For all occasions when conflicts have created problems for Australian diplomacy (Menzies and Casey over Suez in 1956, Fraser and Peacock over Kampuchea in 1980, for example) one can point to happier experiences. Situations vary: particular events and circumstances are determinants.

Australian political leaders have shown an enthusiasm for allowing other amateurs to share in the mysteries of diplomatic endeavour. They have a long tradition of appointing their former political colleagues and other non-professional outsiders to senior diplomatic posts abroad, often to places of particular importance or sensitivity. At the time of writing, the heads of four Australian missions were once politicians: those in Madrid, London, Djakarta and the Hague, while another appointment (to Dublin) has been foreshadowed. In the past other non-foreign service appointments have been made to Washington, Wellington, Paris and Beijing among others.

The reasons governments make such appointments are as varied as the talents of the individuals who have undertaken them. But it is not infrequent for decisions to depend on whether an individual, especially if a practicing or former politician, should be rewarded for services to the party, or removed because of the trouble he or she is causing within it. With such flexible criteria, it is hardly surprising that the success of these appointments has varied. As a former Australian diplomat, Sir Laurence McIntyre observed in 1983, the practice has "been modestly successful; (some) could have done better in a different post; one or two have been near disasters. Perhaps an apt summing up of non-professional diplomacy in general is reflected in the expression "horses for courses".[33] Whatever its merits from a political perspective, this particular system of dispensing patronage, has little attraction for Australia's career diplomats. It may be "part of the system", but appointments generally have a depressing effect on departmental morale even if they do not actually undermine the integrity of the nation's foreign service. But with solid support of most sides of Australian politics, it seems clear that the practice of making amateur appointments will continue, probably with much the same record as in the past.

Political intrusiveness has not only affected the carriage of Australian diplomacy, it has had a lasting impact on methods. In 1911, prime minister Andrew Fisher reject a proposal that dominion High Commissioners resident in London be given modestly increased authority to speak on behalf of their governments because of the precedent it might create; far from home and with the difficulties of communication, commissioners might be tempted to commit their governments to policies for which they did not have authority.[34] Eternally troubled by such a possibility, Australian governments of all political persuasions have been inclined to maintain a tight rein on diplomats in the field. As a result it has rarely been in any officer's interest to show independence or have a line of policy of his or her own, whether serving at home or abroad. The difficulties Australian diplomats face in this regard was the subject of caustic comment in the memoirs of a former Secretary of the Department of Foreign Affairs, Alan Renouf:

> Australia is usually governed by conservative politicians, a lot of whom assume they know everything and think they are particularly adept in foreign policy. The diplomat is not therefore encouraged by many such politicians to make a personal intellectual contribution to foreign policy. Moreover, he becomes aware that to suggest anything to Canberra which may require change in policy may be detrimental to his career ... Hence Australia rarely gets the best value from her diplomats abroad.[35]

As James Eayrs has noted in relation to Canada, strong political control of the foreign services can have other consequences: it tends to discourage initiative, increasing the chances that opportunities for constructive intervention will either be lost, missed or neglected; it discourages public accountability and communication; and overall it encourages diplomats to acquiesce in the general demotion of their place in the conduct of the nation's external affairs.[36] These are not only problems for Canada; they apply with equal force to Australia and are all the more real for the way in which the communications revolution is transforming the conduct of diplomacy around the world.[37]

In general it is evident that developments both at home and abroad are having a damaging impact on the morale of Australia's professional diplomatists. The closing of overseas posts, a decline in the real value of personal overseas allowances and benefits, limited prospects for promotion (now likely to exacerbated by the merger with Trade), a declining perception of foreign affairs as an intellectually challenging and interesting area of public policy and growing political interference, have all served to create this situation. As a result, many senior to middle ranking officers have been leaving the service in recent years, while more junior officers have begun to question the benefits of staying on. In the past, one of the strength of Australia diplomacy has been the professionalism of its career foreign service. Not least of the reasons for Australia enjoying the services of such a generally able and dedicated group of individuals is the reward of a stimulating career. This has long been under threat and there is little doubt that a continuing failure to address the problem of poor morale with Australia's foreign service will ultimately affect the quality of its diplomacy.

Methods and Approaches. Turning from the institutions and practitioners to focus on methods and approaches, one enters an area where generalizations become more problematic. For although academic commentators and practitioners are in broad accord that nations have different methods, and thus have different styles of diplomacy, the characterization of a particular style frequently presents formidable problems. As Stanley Hoffman has pointed out,[38] foreign affairs are managed by limited groups within states; style is, perhaps, not so much a national phenomenon as reflective of elite behaviour; styles change over time—between and within generations, and even the notion of style is illusive—of what is it constituted, for instance?

A nation's diplomatic style should be, it seems, if not unique, then at least distinctive, having been moulded and shaped by local cultural and social values, as well as by the country's foreign interests and international capabilities. In Australia's case this has meant adapting British diplomatic traditions to an antipodean environment. The process was necessarily piecemeal, only gathering momentum as the nation began to pursue a more independent posture in world affairs and as Australians developed a surer sense of their own national identity. It remains, even now, a moot point as to whether Australia has developed a wholly distinctive style of diplomacy, but perhaps the rudiments of a tradition have emerged.

To begin, it is difficult not to agree with Miller and Collins that there is a "commonsense pragmatism" to Australian diplomacy.[39] Frequently, invariably during the most complex negotiations, such as the Third United Nations Conference on the Law of the Sea, Australia has exhibited a desire and seized the initiative in trying to find workable solutions to diplomatically troublesome problems. Equally, one can agree with these authors that Australians show a scepticism about political ideals in so far as they may serve as a foundation for grand designs and ambitions in international affairs. No Australian political leader has ever had the vision or expectation of success to entertain such plans. To most the mere suggestion would have been an effort from a national cultural ethos that proclaims the virtue of common sense (meaning to be practical), and finds pretension in most forms either offensive or risible. Australia it seems, is more a nation of engineers than architects. Yet in Miller's evocative phrase, there is a "dogged low gear idealism" to Australian diplomacy. This is frequently exhibited in determined support for the principles of international law, a commitment to western ideals of justice and equity in international affairs and a respect for, as well as on advocacy of, the rights of small and middle powers in the international system. Translated into an Australian idiom, it means giving people "a fair go".

Leaving pragmatism and idealism to one side, there are still other elements to the Australian style. One is a preference for coalition diplomacy. Successive Australian governments have accepted that for a country such as theirs with limited capabilities in the international arena, this is the most effective way to advance and protect national interests. The practice emerges in various forms—through security dependence on great powers (Britain before the Second World War and the United States in the 1960s), through membership in loose-knit international coalitions during conferences (UNCLOS III) or when pursuing particular objectives (a more equitable international trading system through membership in the "Cairns group" of free traders). Australia has generally shown a preference for quiet diplomacy; the tendency to pursue policy objectives behind closed doors, away from the glare of excessive publicity and public scrutiny. Conservative governments have been particularly anxious to preserve the image of common purpose with Australia's allies and thus been determined to express any criticism of their policies in private and in confidence (Indochina, 1954). Yet it is also true, that political leaders of all persuasions, and occasionally Australia's professional diplomatists, have been vigourously outspoken in defence of Australia's interests and the principles earlier mentioned. Candour and plain spaking, approaching at times a larrikin brashness, has characterized Australian diplomacy (Hughes at Versailles, Evatt at the San Francisco Conference of 1945, Anthony over European protectionism, recent Hawke government commentaries on American and Japanese trade policies). Reflecting, as these qualities do, elements of Australian character, there is often a somewhat self-effacing friendliness and informality to Australian diplomacy. This is in marked contrast to what has been said to be the studied reserve of the British or the presumed air of superiority of the French. It is often the mark of Australia's political diplomatists and is perhaps best personified by Prime Minister Harold Holt's relations with the American president, Lyndon Johnson. This feature of Australian diplomacy has appeared on occasions to lay the foundation for others: as Miller notes, a certain enthusiastic amateurism (Menzies role in the Suez Crisis of 1954), and as John Rowland observes, sporadic "gratuitous acts, the sort of thing ... serious poker players (seek to) avoid."[40] (Holt's recognition of China's nationalist government in 1966, Hayden's 1983 acceptance and subsequent public reporting of Vietnam's (inaccurate) assurances of its troop dispositions in Kampuchea).

In this quest to capture something of the essence of Australia's diplomatic style, it is worth recalling that it owes much to the institutions and practioners discussed earlier. Before the merger of Foreign Affairs and Trade, for example, the divorce between trade and politico-security issues was an elementary feature of Australian diplomacy. It not only produced some of the policy incoherence already mentioned, but a certain diplomatic electicism towards individual countries. Australian diplomatic approaches to Japan, for instance, have often ranged between the hardline tactical maneouvring of the trade negotiator and the more measured accommodating approach of the diplomat. Similarly, the intrusive involvement of politicians in the conduct of diplomacy must be seen as part of the Australian style. On occasions approaches and attitudes have been evident in particular settings or eras. Miller and Mediansky[41] have mentioned, for example, the heavy emphasis on legalism particularly in approaches towards the United Nations. Miller has identified the tendency to elementary collectivism—"the state of mind that looks above all else for inclusive categories" to judge behaviour and actors (communism as expansionist, for example, Asians as part of a single homogeneous culture). Both were features during the long period of postwar coalition governments.

Australian Diplomacy in Asia

What, then, has been the impact of this style of diplomacy on Australia's relations with Asia? At the outset it is useful to underscore the tremendous differences that divide Australia from the countries of the region. Although geographic proximity encourages a perception that Australia is an organic part of Asia, by almost any criteria it is not. As a relatively prosperous European country with liberal democratic political values and a pluralist market economy, Australia's national profile contrasts vividly with even the most westernized and economically advanced of Asia's states. The differences have not only proved an obstacle to understanding; for a long period of time they served as a virtually impenetrable barrier to substantive contact. From an Australian perspective, the legacy of 150 years of proximate living up to the start of the Second World War was little more than a series of perfunctory contacts, racial intolerance, ignorance of custom and culture, fear and hostility.[42]

As Asia's political and economic importance began to be appreciated after 1945, attitudes began to change, Australia began building substantive cooperative relationships with the countries of the region. Even so, the transition to closer contact, let alone undestanding and cooperation, has been slow. The prewar legacy had to be overcome, but Australia's early postwar foreign policy towards Asia was also a constraint. Conceived against the background of a perceived hegemonial communist threat to Asia and cast in the mold of its great power allies, Britain and the United States, Australia stood, for nearly 20 years, in their shadow. The effect was not only to obscure to Australians the reality of a set of national interests in Asia independent of those claimed by their allies, but to mask to Asian governments and their people, Australia's distinctive regional interests and its wish for closer contact. It was only towards the end of the Vietnam War, as London and Washington began their military withdrawal from the Asian mainland, as Australia ended its own pathological preoccupation with the communist threat, and as the countries of Southeast Asia in particular showed strong signs of political stability and a measure of economic prosperity, that the prospect for better relations between Australia and its Asian neighbours emerged.

The institutions of Australian diplomacy, most notably the Department of Foreign Affairs, were slow to adjust to postwar changes in attitudes towards Asia.[43] Created and nurtured against a background of British, or more generally European and western influences from within Australian society, and designed to serve a decidedly Eurocentric foreign policy Australia's foreign service was founded on the European model. Everything about its structure, organizational processes, the focus of its interests, the recruitment and training of its personnel and its commitment to particular forms of expertise, such as European language training, reflected the fact. To break down the deeply entrenched attitudes that sustained this entirely natural bias, to change the *weltanschauung* of the Australian foreign service to reflect, essentially for the first time, the imperatives of a foreign policy focused on Asia, proved a long and excruciatingly slow process. One powerful reason was Foreign Affair's commitment to generalism, which largely precluded the rapid acquisition of expertise in Asian affairs and thus the development of policies based on an informed and intelligent understanding of the forces that moved them.

Space does not permit Australia's diplomatic relationships with Asian countries to be explored in detail. Suffice, perhaps, to be selective and to suggest the broad outlines of Canberra's postwar approach in each of Asia's three subregions, beginning in the west and moving east.

South Asia. Shared membership of the Commonwealth notwithstanding, relations between Australia and the countries of South Asia—India, Pakistan, Sri Lanka and Bangladesh—have never been particularly close. After three of the four gained their independence in the late 1940s, Australia's contributions to economic development through participation in the Colombo Plan led largely to functional aid relationships. In the case of India and Sri Lanka (Ceylon at the time) these later developed into more testing political relationships as the governments of the two countries embraced neutralism while Australia followed its more powerful western allies and moved decisively towards anti-communism. During the long period of conservative party rule in Australia, relations between India and Australia were especially difficult. On the other hand, Pakistan's sympathy for American policy led to Islamabad and Canberra becoming joint members of the ill-fated Southeast Asia Treaty Organization.

Since the early 1970s efforts have been made to place Australian-South Asian relations on a firmer basis, but foundations are difficult to discover. Thus far opportunities of expanded trade links have proved limited. New Delhi's close links to Moscow have made conservative governments in

Australia particularly wary. The wretched state of the Bangladesh economy and political instability there have served as impediments to all substantive contacts beyond Canberra providing a useful source of foreign aid. Military rule in Pakistan, with perceived concomitant abuses of human rights among other points of disagreement, has limited bilateral contacts with Islamabad. Finally, cross-cutting political tensions among the states of the region make South Asia a difficult place for Australia to try to develop a coherent regional foreign policy and for the most part Canberra has not attempted to do so.

Thus for most of the period since 1945 South Asia has been a relatively low priority region for Australian foreign policy. One consequence is that the intrusive diplomatic style of Australian governments has been less in evidence in South Asia than anywhere else in the Asian arena: for the most part Australia's foreign service has accepted the burden of managing relations. There have been periods where this has been less so; Casey, as foreign minister, for example, made periodic visits to the region;[44] Whitlam sought new foundations for closer contract, while a previous foreign minister, Mr Hayden, made an extensive visit in 1985 as part of an Indian Ocean thrust in his policies. But often it has seemed that the regular meetings of Commonwealth leaders have provided sufficient opportunities for contact and consultation. Thus the tendency for the Australian government to favour multilateral areas for diplomatic discourse has been much in evidence. The results have been mixed. Policy differences, but also differing diplomatic styles, set Menzies and Nehru at odds with one another;[45] on the other hand, prime ministers Hawke and Rajiv Gandhi apparently established a warm personal relationship which produced profitable exchanges and cooperation over an issue such as apartheid in South Africa.[46] Occasionally, events such as the periodic wars between India and Pakistan, or the Tamil separatist problem in Sri Lanka have confronted Australia with potentially difficult regional issues. That these have rarely proved awkward or especially challenging to Canberra may be a reflection of diplomatic skills, but with few direct or clearly defined interests in the region, Australia has also not been forced to make policy-decisions which might expose its weaknesses.

Southeast Asia. In Southeast Asia by contrast, the challenges for Australian diplomacy have and will continue to be considerable. As in South Asia many of the countries of the region face profound internal economic, political and social problems which they are being forced to confront against a background of regional tensions. While the ideological chasm between the western oriented states of the Association of Southeast Asian Nations (ASEAN), and the socialist countries of Indochina is most obvious, economic and political harmony among the ASEAN six seems an increasingly tarnished ideal. For Australian policy makers the significance of all this is that unlike in South Asia, they are confronted by difficulties and dilemmas in a region where their country's interests are directly and inextricably engaged. Reflecting this interest, Australian governments have been attempting to turn the postwar rhetoric of Southeast Asia's importance to Australia into something more substantive.

The profoundly complex nature of this task has been underscored in recent years by a succession of bilateral confrontations between Australia and many of its Southeast Asian neighbours—a dispute with Malaysia over Australian education policy, with Singapore over international airline policy, with the Philippines over foreign aid, with Vietnam over Kampuchea, and with Indonesia over all manner of issues, including human rights in East Timor, Australia security policy and freedom of the media.[47]

As each of these examples testifies, specific policy issues have the capacity to disrupt Australia's bilateral relationships in Southeast Asia. But they have often proved more serious because of the way in which they have been handled. To some regional governments Australian diplomacy in Southeast Asia has often seemed inept. A recent case in point was foreign minister Bill Hayden's 1983 efforts to engineer a settlement of the Kampuchean issues. The enterprise foundered on various shoals but is remembered here for the considerable criticism Hayden earned from ASEAN governments. His efforts were seen as ill-conceived, pretentious for a country of Australia's size and status and, more to the point, an invasion of ASEAN's presumed foreign policy prerogatives. At the same time, Hayden was thought to show himself as untutored in the ways of Asian diplomacy by the candour of some of his public statements and as naive in his acceptance and trust of Vietnamese policy assurances.[48] The point underscored by the episode was not so much that Australia has policy differences with its neighbours—that is almost to be expected—but rather the pitfalls of Australia attempting to conduct diplomacy in a milieu where it is very much a cultural outsider. On this as on other issues, the style of Australian diplomacy was viewed as abrasive, amateurish, high handed and thus counter-productive.

Australia's diplomatic problems in Southeast Asia are nowhere more evident than in Canberra's relations with Djakarta. Indeed, Alan Renouf has characterized the relationship as the crucible of Australian foreign policy.[49] Founded on relatively good relations following Australia's support for Indonesian independence in the late 1940's the relationship since then has oscillated between military confrontation and harmonious cooperation, with a mean somewhere around wary accommodation. Sporadic policy differences have often accounted for these fluctuations, but Canberra has been largely unable to decide on a suitable formula for the conduct of its relationship with Indonesia. Over four decades various approaches have been tried, modified and then abandoned. Clearly the problems emanate from both sides of the relationship, but from Canberra's perspective, many have their roots in being uncertain of how to deal with a country whose welfare, social order, legal and political systems are so fundamentally different from its own.[50]

That this has proved so difficult exposes a fundamental dilemma for Australian diplomacy in Southeast Asia. Australians need to become part of Asia, but do they need to become Asian to do so, or can they achieve this aim retaining their western identity? As an unnamed Malaysian foreign ministry official was reported to have said in 1983, "Australians are far too conscious of their white skins ever to become part of this (Southeast Asia) region''.[51] The individual concerned was not apparently referring to the racial overtones that have sometimes accompanied Australia's approach to the area, but rather to Austral self-conscious awareness of being a European outpost located on Asia's vast periphery. In times past this has caused insecurity, an apprehension that lingers, but more important, in the present context, is the barrier it constitutes to better relations. Preoccupied with the differences between European and Asians, between their natural loyalties and ties to the west and all that is alien in Asia, Australians and their governments have often seemed to lack the motivation to search conscientiously for the mutual points of contact and complementary interests that might better serve the end of cooperation. Instead diplomacy has often been palliative, designed to relieve the anxiety of alienation, but never to address its causes.

Yet it is a mark of the desire for better relations on both sides that Australia and its ASEAN neighbours have developed some specific diplomatic mechanisms to promote better contacts and understanding. Canberra's participation (as a dialogue partner with other Asian-Pacific states) in the annual ASEAN Post-Ministerial Conference is the most important, but in addition there is an ASEAN-Australian Forum and the ASEAN-Australian Consultative Meeting. Australian aid to ASEAN states is facilitated by way of the ASEAN-Australian Economic Cooperation Program. Overall, however, Australian diplomacy in Southeast Asia has lacked sureness of touch. Some of Canberra's more creative ventures, such as its 1983 efforts over Kampuchea have not only not succeeded, they have been harmful to Australia's interests, at least among ASEAN states. At the same time, the effective management of day to day issues has frequently been undercut by mutual misunderstandings stemming from fundamentally different value systems. This and the political economic and social diversity of the region, sufficient of itself to create deep cleavages among local powers, presents Australian diplomatists with an exceedingly demanding regional agenda.

East Asia. Australia's principal foreign policy relationships in this area are with the Peoples' Republic of China and Japan. After the success of China's communist revolution in 1949, Beijing and Canberra did not establish diplomatic relations until 1973. In the interim, Australian political leaders viewed China as a pariah state of international politics and took every opportunity to criticize its communist government and the allegedly destabilizing nature of its foreign policy. Yet this did not entirely preclude contacts between the two countries. Australian attitudes towards China in the 1950s and the 1960s serve as a useful example of Canberra's tendency, mentioned earlier, to separate the commercial and political elements of its external policy and of the incoherence this can cause. For while refusing to recognise Mao Tse Tung's communist government and accusing it of being the motivating force behind Hanoi's aggression in South Vietnam (where Australian military forces were fighting), Canberra nevertheless conducted an active and lucrative wheat trade with the Chinese. The inconsistency in these policies frequently embarrassed

Liberal-Country party governments as they attempted to justify their policies in Vietnam, and they helped to undermine the Department of Foreign Affairs' efforts to assert greater bureaucratic control over external policy.[52]

Once formal diplomatic contact was established, the relationship expanded steadily. Whitlam's personal overtures towards Beijing before becoming prime minister and his desire to maintain their momentum afterwards, served as the foundation for a firm friendship. A distinguished Australian sinologist, Dr S. Fitzgerald, rather than a foreign service nominee, was appointed Australia's first ambassador and early attempts were made to expand the range of economic and cultural contacts. All subsequent Australian governments, not least that of the conservative Mr. Fraser have made good relations with China a pillar of their foreign policy in Asia.[53] To that end, the present prime minister has continued to follow his two immediate predecessors in taking a strong personal interest in the relationship, seeking to promote it by active personal diplomacy. At the same time China's long term significance to Australia has been underscored by the creation of similar specialized diplomatic mechanisms to promote closer contacts as has been done in relation to ASEAN. The Australia-China Council, for example, is designed to foster scientific cultural and educational exchanges between the two countries and has proved a useful medium for extending areas of cooperation. Although some Australians hold unrealistic expectations about the economic benefits to be had from China's program of modernization, it seems clear that the apparently mutual desire for further contacts built around complementary economic interests in service, resource, and to a lesser extent manufacturing industries, will lead to a wider, more complex functional relationship. In the meantime, China's growing political presence in the Asia-Pacific region may provide Canberra with a succession of diplomatic challenges as it seeks to relate that presence to its own existing and developing interests in the area.[54]

If Australia's relations with China show potential for expansion and also present challenges, no less is true of its relationship with Japan. But here future developments will take place against the background of a warm and mutually beneficial economic relationship stretching back over several decades. It is a reflection of the existing strength and importance of this relationship that Australia's embassy in Tokyo is already the second largest of its overseas missions after Washington. That it is also an increasingly multifaceted relationship is reflected in the wide range of federal ministries represented in the mission.

Australia's postwar relationship with Japan began inauspiciously as Canberra took a hard line on Tokyo's aggressive wartime policies in the Pacific. But after insisting on a punitive peace settlement that would put an end to Japanese militarism, the Menzies government eventually accepted Washington's more liberal approach. Less than a decade later (in 1957) the two countries signed the Trade Agreement which served as the foundation for a remarkably close cooperative economic relationship.[55] Over the next two decades Japan's burgeoning capacity as a producer and exporter of manufactured goods, and Australia's development of export-oriented mining and mineral resource industries provided the foundations for an economic partnership that eventually saw Japan become the principal customer for Australian mineral export and Australia the principal source of Japan's energy imports. Over the past decade the supplier—consumer relationship which once formed the central motif of the Australian-Japan relationship has been changing. The reasons, of course, are complex and cannot be explored in detail here; suffice to say that economic pressures both at home (in Japan and Australia) and abroad, particularly in the form of protectionism in the United States and Europe at a time of internationally weak commodity markets, as well as changes in Japan's political role in world affairs, have all contributed. Economic ties remain the core of the relationship, but they are being spread across a wider range of activities; in addition to a more modest trade in the supply of energy resources, they include an expansion of Japanese tourism to Australia, joint ventures in fields such as motor car manufacture and resort development and Japanese participation in the Australian banking industry.

The structure of the Australian-Japanese relationship has made special demands on Australian diplomacy. First, it is worthwhile noting that the singular importance of Japan to Australia's continued economic prosperity has required its management at the highest political levels. While Australia's professional diplomats have managed the day-to-day business of the relationship, strong ministerial involvement has been a persistent fact of life. Nor has this been confined merely to the prime minister and the foreign minister. Although both have always been active participants, the highly functional nature of the relationship has meant widespread involvement by ministers holding a diverse range of portfolios, most notably those with responsibilities in the areas of primary industry, trade, finance, tourism and secondary industry. As a corollary this has also meant the extensive involvement of federal departments of state other than foreign affairs in the conduct of relations. The need for internal mechanisms of policy coordination has thus been at a premium.

The special importance of the relationship also led to the creation of various specialized policy advisory units and consultative councils to facilitate decision-making and dialogue. A Japan secretariat within the Department of Foreign Affairs and Trade is designed to provide specialized policy advice and a mechanism for policy coordination, and an Australian-Japan Council with a brief to promote exchanges and contacts in the manner of the Australian-China Council also exists. Direct government-to-government communications have been facilitated by annual ministerial consultations, while in 1976 the whole relationship was brought under an umbrella accord with potentially wide-ranging implications through The Basic Treaty of Friendship and Cooperation.[56]

It is also worth pointing out that Australia's relationship with Japan is among the most important for the governments of the states.[57] During the 1960s and 70s contacts built around resource-based industries provided a natural foundation for the states to become parties to Australian diplomacy since it was they who owned the minerals and regulated their exploitation. Thus, Queensland, Western Australia and New South Wales have all maintained active diplomatic contacts with Japan through the establishment of representative offices in Tokyo and frequent ministerial visits. Whatever the benefits of these activities from the perspective of the states, they complicate the task of coordinating and representing Australian interests in Japan. The point was made in the Myer report in 1979. "Australia's federal system", Myer argued,

> impinges on relations with Japan in two interrelated ways. First it reinforces Japan's impression of Australia as a country lacking cohesion and broad consensus on national direction, particularly in basic policy areas such as foreign investment, universal and energy resource development and industrial growth. Secondly, the Japanese are placed in a position of being able to derive advantage from playing the states off against one another or the states against the Commonwealth.[58]

Australia's relationship with Japan has been a demanding one to manage, not least because of the differences in the societies. Negotiation over beef, coal and iron ore prices, for example, have always been tough and there have been moments of tension as during the 1976 sugar row. But in general, the underlying complementarity of the two countries' interests facilitates a sound cooperative relationship. At the moment, these foundations are shifting and the basis of the relationship changing. In recent months this has been reflected in the increasingly shrill, critical and candid way that Australian leaders, from the Prime Minister down, have been speaking about Japan's international trade policy. Canberra's relations with Tokyo remain sound, and appear to be on the verge of entering a new era. but it seems almost certain that it too will be one which will demand more of Australian diplomacy than in the past.

Conclusion

Reviewing nearly nine decades of Australian diplomacy it is difficult not to see the landmark developments as being anything other than a series of ad hoc responses to momentary pressures or problems. Not for Australians during the early part of the century were notions that a foreign office separate from the other departments of state was a necessary adjunct to nationhood, or that an independent foreign service was an indispensable symbol of sovereignty in world affairs. In the evolution of Australia's diplomatic institutions, abstract ideas focussed on the theoretically possible or the notionally desirable failed to be as persuasive as the pragmatically necessary. Thus the protection of Australian interests as a dominion within the imperial system demanded diplomatic skills, but they could be found within a relatively crude administrative framework; Australia did not have need for or wish to pay the cost of its own diplomatic representatives when Britain already had an extensive network of legations around the world. An independent foreign ministry only became necessary in 1935 through a series of international crisis; opening diplomatic contacts in the Pacific in 1939 was a response to Japan's belligerency; confronting the reality of Asia was a legacy of war, and so on.

To the extent that many of these developments, or not, as the case may be, are explicable by reference to Australia's place within the Empire, they have a coherence or thematic rationale. But if there was a grander design behind these moves, or once again, an absence of one, it was wonderfully surreal. In reality there was not. The evolution of Australian diplomacy might be viewed as steady progress towards greater sophistication and institutionalization, consonant with Australia's hesitant movement towards greater autonomy in global affairs, but this is far from the case. Rather it took place through a series of moves, many forward, some back, others laterally, depending on events both at home and abroad.

In an environment so seemingly inhospitable to plans and designs, still less theory, the prospect of discovering some underlying principles or coherent assumptions in Australia's diplomatic methods, might reasonably seem remote. Yet one can see its promise in the persisting traditions of Australian diplomacy, in recurring patterns of behaviour and in the commitment to certain values. The characteristics of busy amateurism, prime ministerial preeminence, diplomatic rotation, management generalism, pragmatism and coalition building, *et al.* testify to it. That these are not the product of a specific, self-consciously articulated theory of diplomacy is hardly in doubt. Yet they do seem to reflect assumptions on the part of the Australian people, or more aptly, those elites largely responsible for the conduct of their external relations, about their nation's place and role in the world. For example, seeing the international environment as hostile and Australia as at best a middle power with widely spread interests; placing a premium on evolutionary change and on the mechanisms of diplomacy, international law, broad based inter-governmental organizations and multilateral activities as means of securing and maintaining order. These might, perhaps, be core assumptions which help explain the cast of Australian diplomacy.

Whether Australian diplomacy, overall, is effective, whether its methods and institutions are functional and well adapted to the nations's foreign policy needs and wether its practitioners are sufficiently skilled to meet effectively the challenges of the contemporary international environment are issues too large to address in detail here. But reviewing them in generality, in relation to Asia, it is clear that given the point from which it began 40 or thereabouts years ago, the effort Australia has put into its diplomatic relationships in Asia is little short of remarkable. Starting with a few small scattered missions in places like New Delhi, Singapore and Nanking in the 1940s, Australia is now represented in nearly every Asian capital. More of Australia's diplomatic resources go to serving these posts than to any other region.

It is doubtful, however, whether conscientiousness alone is enough. Despite the scale of its efforts, Australia is still a relatively new diplomatic actor in Asia as is all too evident when seemingly manageable policy problems become sources of irritation and tension. Canberra's busiest amateurs—its politicians—seem especially prone to unhappy adventure in parts of Asia, though it is not true of all, as Casey was able to show. On occasion Canberra has been imaginative in its approach to this demanding diplomatic environment—the creation of special forums like the Australian-Japan Ministerial Committee as mechanisms for dialogue, being an example. At other times, as when Foreign Affairs began to turn its attentions rather ponderously towards Asia in the 1950s, creativity has been lacking. It is, however, extremely difficult to generalize now that the range of Australia's contacts with Asian countries has become so vast. The record, as one might expect, is extremely mixed. In Japan, Australia's particular style of diplomacy has facilitated a close, generally harmonious bilateral relationship; in Indonesia, by contrast, the result has been alarmingly counter-productive and has often had the opposite effect. There is no simple, ready explanation for these startling contrasts, just as there is none for the many variations on these themes which can be seen in Australia's other diplomatic relationships in Asia. Relations rest on complex calculations of interest. It may be a function of diplomacy, and a measure of its success, to be able to harmonize these calculations, but ultimately relations between states are at the mercy of other forces. However well-crafted to the perceived demands of any given situation, diplomacy can only ever do so much.

NOTES

1 See W. J. Hudson, *Billy Hughes in Paris The Birth of Australian Diplomacy* (Melbourne: Thomas Nelson, 1978).
2 Quoted in P. G. Edwards, *Prime Ministers and Diplomats The Making of Australian Foreign Policy 1901-1949* (Melbourne: Oxford University Press, 1983), p. 1.
3 According to one account Australians had "opinions about foreign policy, but no foreign policy as such". See Norman Harper and David Sissons, *Australia and the United Nations* (New York: Manhattan Publications, 1959), p. 30.
4 For a good discussion of these, see Edwards, *Prime Minister and Diplomats*.
5 *Ibid.*, pp. 3-4.
6 See T. B. Millar, *Australia in Peace and War External Relations 1788-1977* (Canberra: Australian National University Press, 1978), pp. 74-6.
7 See Hudson, *Billy Hughes in Paris*, ch. 1.
8 Quoted in Robert Clyde Toennessen, "An Analysis of the Changing Bases of Australian Foreign Policy" (Ph.D. dissertation, The American University, 1971). p. 148.
9 See Edwards, *Prime Ministers and Diplomats*, esp. ch. 3.
10 *Ibid.*, p. 82-3.
11 A department of External Affairs had been created at the time of federation and the portfolio held by the prime minister.
12 For a discussion of Australian policy during this period, see Paul Hasluck, *The Government and the People 1939-1941*, vol. Number 4 in the series *Australia in the War of 1939-1945* (Canberra: Australian War Memorial, 1952).
13 Quoted in Alan Watt, *The Evolution of Australian Foreign Policy 1938-1965* (Cambridge: Cambridge University Press, 1967), p. 24. As a result of this decision Australia opened diplomatic contacts with the United States, Japan and China. See Edwards *Prime Ministers and Diplomats*, pp. 116-30.

14 These events are discussed in Christopher Thorne, *Allies of a Kind* (Oxford: Oxford University Press, 1979), ch. 9; Roger J. Bell, *Unequal Alies Australian-American Relations and the Pacific War* (Melbourne: Melbourne University Press, 1977) and D. M. Horner, *High Command, Australian and Allied Strategy 1939-1945* (Sydney: George Allen and Unwin, 1982).
15 P. G. Edwards, "The origins and growth of professional diplomacy in Australia", Australian Foreign Affairs Review, 56:11, (November 1985), p. 1075.
16 *Ibid.*, p. 1076.
17 This is a very clearly defined theme in Edwards, *Prime Ministers and Diplomats*.
18 For a wider discussion of the points that follow, see Hugh Collins, "Challenges and Options for the Department of Foreign Affairs in its fiftieth year", *Australian Foreign Affairs Review*, 56:11 (November 1985), pp. 1077-89.
19 For a discussion, see Hugh Collins, "Federalism and Australia's External Relations", *Australian Outlook*, 29:2 (August 1985), pp. 123-76.
20 The department was initially called External Affairs. In 1970 its name was changed to Foreign Affairs. As of July 1987, it has become the Department of Foreign Affairs and Trade.
21 See Edwards, *Prime Ministers and Diplomats*, ch. 1.
22 One of the most formidable was also among the most recent: Malcolm Fraser's propriety interest in foreign policy during his premiership between 1975 and 1983 led to a steady drift in power away from the department towards the prime minister's office. For a discussion, see Alan Renouf, *Malcolm Fraser and Australian Foreign Policy* (Sydney: Australian Professional Publications, 1986), vh. 5.
23 The early development of federal department is discussed in R. P. Deare, *The Establishment of the Department of Trade* (Canberra: Australian National University, 1963). On the subject of Australia's early trade representation overseas, see Millar, *Australia in Peace and War*, esp. Appendix C.
24 For a discussion of the decision at the time, see Russell Trood, "Uneasy alliance of trade and diplomacy", *Sydney Morning Herald*, 18 August 1987.
25 Collins, "Challenges and Options", p. 1084.
26 The difficulties are discussed in Hugh Collins, "The 'Coombs Report': Bureaucracy, Diplomacy and Australian Foreign Policy", *Australian Outlook*, 30:31 (December 1976), pp. 387-413.
27 Collins, "Challenges and Options", p. 1087.
28 Gregory Clark, "Vietnam, China and the foreign affairs debate in Australia: a personal account", in *Australia's Vietnam*, ed. Peter King (Sydney: George Allen and Unwin, 1983), ch. 2 at p. 31 Also see Clark's "The Australian Department of Foreign Affairs—What's Wrong with our Diplomats", *The Australian Quarterly*, 47:2 (June 1975), pp. 21-35.
29 See Arthur M. Schlesinger, Jr., "A Thousand Days", *John F. Kennedy in the White House* (Boston: Houghton Mifflin, 1965), p. 408-9.
30 Quoted in Alan Reid, *The Gorton Experiment* (Sydney: Shakespeare Press, 1971), p. 55.
31 Quoted in Edwards, *Prime Ministers and Diplomats*, p. 6-7.
32 On Chifley's approach, see L. F. Crisp, *Ben Chifley* (Sydney: Longmans) On Whitlam's see Henry S. Albinski, *Australian External Policy Under Labor* (St Lucia: University of Queensland Press, 1977).
33 Sir Laurence McIntrye, "Reflections on Australian Diplomacy", in *Independence and Alliance Australia in World Affairs 1976-80*, eds., P. J. Boyce and J. D. Angel (Sydney: George Allen and Unwin, 1983) p. 315.
34 Edwards, *Prime Ministers and Diplomats*, pp. 19-20.
35 Alan Renouf, *The Champagne Trail* (Melbourne: Sun books, 1980) p. 134.
36 James Eayrs, *The Art of the Possible, Government and Foreign Policy in Canada* (Toronto: University of Toronto Press, 1961), pp. 174-75.
37 See Adam Watson, *Diplomacy. The Dialogue Between States* (London: Methuen, 1982), ch. 4.
38 Stanley Hoffman, *Gullivers Troubles, or the Setting of American Foreign Policy* (New York: McGraw-Hill, 1968), pp. 87-8.

39 J. D. B. Miller, "The Conduct of Australian Foreign Policy", *The Australian University*, 7:2, pp. 134-58 at pp. 138-38 and Collins, "Challenges and Options", p. 1081. Many of the other elements mentioned by Miller have been referred to as well.
40 John Rowland, "Some Reflections on Australian Foreign Policy", Unpublished seminar paper, delivered in the Department of Political Science, The Australian National University, August 1984, p. 17.
41 Miller, p. 138 and F. A. Mediansky, "The Conservative Style in Australian Foreign Policy", *Australian Outlook*, 28:1 (April 's 74), pp. 50-56.
42 For an overview, see Werner Levi, *Australia's Outlook on Asia* (Sydney: Angus and Robertson, 1958).
43 See Clark's works referred to in note 28.
44 For an insight into his diplomacy, see T. B. Miller, ed., *Australian Foreign Minister. The Diaries of R. G. Casey 1951-60* (London: Collins, 1972).
45 See Mediansky, "The Conservative Style".
46 *The Bulletin*, 14 October 1986.
47 These are just same of the issues that have arisen over the last decade or so. To gain a feel for relations, see J. R. Angel, "Australia and South-East Asia", in Boyce and Angel, eds., *Independence and Alliance*, ch. 14.
48 See *Canberra Times*, 18 November 1983, *The Weekend Australian*, 1-2 October 1983.
49 Alan Renouf, *The Frightened Country* (Sydney: Macmillan, 1979), p. 399.
50 For various views of Australia's relations with Indonesia, see the special edition of *Australian Outlook*, 40:3, (December 1986).
51 Reported by M. A. Razman, *Sydney Morning Herald*, 28 November 1983.
52 See John Reynolds, "Recognition by Trade: The Controversial Wheat Sales to China", *Australian Outlook*, 18:2 (August 1964), pp. 117-26.
53 Australia's relations during the Whitlam and Fraser eras are discussed in Albinski, *Australian External Policy* and Renouf, *Malcolm Fraser and Australian Policy*.
54 See G. S. R. Wood, "Australia's Trading Relations with East Asia" in Paul Dibb ed., *Australia's External Relations in the 1980s* (Canberra, Croom Helm, 1983), ch. 10.
55 The negotiation of the treaty is examined in Alan Rix, *Coming to Terms. The politics of Australia's trade with Japan, 1945-57* (Sydney: Allen and Unwin, 1986).
56 For a discussion of these points, see Alan Rix, "Australia and East Asia, Japan", in Boyce and Angel, eds., *Independence and Alliance*, ch. 12, esp. p. 205.
57 This dimension of the relationship is examined in Peter Drysdale and Hirofuna Shibata, *Federalism and Resource Development* (Sydney: George Allen and Unwin, 1985).
58 Quoted in John Warhurst and Gillian O'Loghlin, "Federal-State issues in external economic relations", in *ibid.*, p. 192.

ASEAN Diplomacy: National Interest and Regionalism

LAU TEIK SOON*

ABSTRACT

ASEAN diplomacy reveals an interplay between national interest and regionalism among ASEAN states. Indonesia's President Suharto is a major force in ASEAN because of Indonesia's emphasis on consensual decision-making. ASEAN diplomatic ideas and practices stress mutual respect, national development and economic cooperation, cultural cooperation and national identity, and finally security cooperation.

THE ASSOCIATION OF SOUTHEAST ASIAN NATIONS or ASEAN as its name implies is an association of six independent and sovereign states, viz., Brunei, Indonesia, Malaysia, the Philippines, Singapore and Thailand. It was founded in August 1967[1] and in January 1984 Brunei became its sixth member.[2] Burma, Cambodia, Laos and Vietnam had been invited to attend the Annual Meeting of Foreign Ministers by the host government at various times but none of them has considered applying for membership in the regional organization. ASEAN, therefore, has yet to establish itself as an international organization acceptable to all the governments in Southeast Asia.

ASEAN was originally conceived as a convenient compromise to meet common challenges, particularly those arising from the external environment, rather than as a panacea for national problems. Indeed, the member states adopt different regional perspectives based on their national interests and espouse merely rhetorical programmes of cooperation at times. Nonetheless, they have also expressed a collective commitment to achieving a regional entity with a supranational authority. Through patience, endurance and commitment, the ASEAN governments have made significant progress towards regional unification.[3]

A study of ASEAN thus serves to highlight the interplay between national interest and regionalism.[4] There are three other reasons why such a study would be useful. Firstly, each member state of ASEAN has retained its unique national characteristics and policy principles in spite of active participation in the ASEAN diplomacy. Secondly, ASEAN countries constitute a fast-growing economic region: Singapore is classified as a newly industrialized country or NIC and some of the other members, particularly Thailand, are on course to

* Department of Political Science, National University of Singapore.

join the ranks of the NICs. Thirdly, although each state pursues its own foreign policy, a remarkable degree of collaboration on various international issues has been achieved, particularly those relating to the Cambodian problem. Every member government regards regionalism as the cornerstone of its foreign policy. Thus, the ASEAN diplomacy has served both the national interest and regionalism: this balance of interests has been the most striking characteristic of ASEAN's diplomatic practice.

Equality of States

When ASEAN was established, its members subscribed to certain basic principles: respect for independence, sovereignty; territorial integrity; non-interference in the internal affairs of member states; peaceful settlement of dispute and cooperation for mutual benefit. More significantly, the equality of the member states was upheld, regardless of the difference in their political and socio-economic systems. In practice, however, there exists a hierarchy of states in terms of power and influence.

The biggest state of ASEAN, Indonesia, initially had serious political differences with its neighbours, Malaysia and Singapore. The issue concerned its regional leadership. Under President Sukarno, Indonesia sought regional leadership in an expanded archipelago termed the "Greater Indonesia" or "Indonesia Raya" which would dominate the neighbouring states. When the British imperialists supported the formation of Malaysia which would incorporate the Malay Peninsula, Singapore and the Borneo territories, President Sukarno objected on the ground that he was not consulted. To placate Indonesia, the Prime Minister of Malaya, Tengku Abdul Rahman, met President Sukarno and President Macapagal of the Philippines, with whom the Tengku discussed the Philippines' claim over the territory of Sabah.

A diplomatic agreement was reached to form the MAPHILINDO,[5] the regional organisation which would embrace the Malay ethnic-based states of Malaysia, Philippines and Indonesia.[6] This narrowly-based and misguided concept, however, foundered on the rocks of the Tengku's impatience and Sukarno's grandiose ambition. When the Tengku declared the formation of Malaysia, on 16 September, 1963, President Sukarno protested that this was tantamount to a breach of the Tengku's earlier undertaking. Sukarno's policy of *Confrontasi* was a mix of loud threats, ill-planned incursions by land and air and badly organized naval and trade blockade. It led partly to his downfall after the abortive coup by the Indonesian Communist Party in September 1965.

With the advent of President Suharto, Indonesia embarked on a diplomatic course which was to see it assume a regional leadership role acceptable to the neighbouring states. Suharto initiated the "good neighbour policy" which consists of three main components: pursuance of cordial bilateral relations, commitment to regional unification and the settlement of regional conflicts. Suharto ended the confrontation between Indonesia on the one hand and

Malaysia and Singapore on the other. Subsequently, extensive ties in the diplomatic, economic, cultural and security fields were established. Today, Indonesia has excellent relations with its immediate neighbours.

Most importantly, Indonesia initiated the formation of ASEAN.[7] Soon after the normalisation talks between Indonesia and Malaysia, Thanat Khoman (Thai Foreign Minister) suggested to Adam Malik (Indonesian Foreign Minister) that it was an opportune moment in history to form a new regional organization. Thereafter, Malik and his emissaries sounded out all of the governments in Southeast Asia except North and South Vietnam which were then in the midst of their civil wars. In August 1967, five states agreed to the formation of ASEAN.

The success of ASEAN thus far owes much to the commitment of President Suharto who, despite the nationalistic view that Indonesia should assert its leadership role, has always insisted on consensual decision-making by ASEAN. The best example of this is the debate over the Cambodian problem. Even at times when the patience of Indonesian diplomatic and military officials was sorely tested, President Suharto remained committed to the unity and cohesion of ASEAN.

Indonesia has also taken the initiative to solve other bilateral and regional conflicts. The ending of the "Confrontasi" policy is an example. Then about three years later, Indonesian Foreign Minister Adam Malik had to display his statesmanship and Indonesia's "good neighbour policy" by refraining from aggressive reaction to the Singaporean execution of the Indonesian marines found guilty of sabotage and murder. In 1968, Malik mediated in the dispute between Malaysia and the Philippines which had resulted in a deadlock of the activities of ASEAN and even threatened the continued existence of the regional organization. Besides, Indonesia also took the initiative in proposing a Nuclear Weapon Free Zone (NWFZ) for the ASEAN region.[8]

Indonesia has been unanimously accepted as the leader of ASEAN in regional affairs. This is testified by a number of ASEAN's decisions, which include the locating of the ASEAN Secretariat in Jakarta, the appointment of an Indonesian as the first Secretaty General of ASEAN, the holding of the first ASEAN Summit in Bali and the recognition of President Suharto as the elder statesman in Southeast Asia.

Indonesia may assume that, as the largest ASEAN state, it should have dominant influence over regional matters. But such an assumption applies equally to the other large states in ASEAN. For example, Malaysia also felt the "bullying tactics" of Confrontasi of Indonesia. The Tengku had to accommodate Sukarno's pressure to postpone the establishment of Malaysia and to accept the UN mediation. When the Indonesia-Malaysian rapprochement to form the MAPHILINDO broke down, the Tengku had to rely on the Commonwealth-ANZUK powers to defend the country against the military incursions of Indonesia.

As the smallest state of ASEAN, Singapore and Brunei share equally the common concern of external interference, by other ASEAN states, in their domestic affairs. Since Singapore became independent in August 1965, it has protested against numerous instances of Malaysian interference in its internal affairs. The period 1965-1968 was particularly difficult for Singapore as it made the adjustment to becoming independent. This adjustment crisis was manifested in the plenitude of disputes over economic, trade, immigration and defence issues during the period. Even today, Singapore cannot help but be wary of the interference of Malaysian pressure groups which are officially sanctioned. The visit in 1986 by President Herzog of Israel to Singapore was regarded as an affront by the Muslims in Malaysia. The ensuing widespread demonstrations against the Singapore government were conducted chiefly by the Islamic groups, both inside and outside the Malaysian government circles.

Singapore's decision to go ahead with the Israeli President's visit demonstrated the political will of the government to not succumb to pressures from Malaysia. Such political will was also evident when the Singapore government went ahead with the execution of the Indonesian marines in 1968, despite the appeals by both President Suharto and the Malaysian Prime Minister. The temporary withholding of support by Singapore for Indonesia's incorporation of East Timor was another testimony of the sensitivity of smaller ASEAN states to the attempts at regional dominance by the neighbours.

Brunei is similarly worried about the dominance of Indonesia and Malaysia in the region.[9] Such fears are heightened as a result of the Brunei-Sarawak dispute over the territory in Limbang. Although Brunei shares common cultural, linguistic and religious backgrounds with Malaysia, it is constantly vigilant against Malaysian interference. The problem was once aggravated by Malaysia's harbouring of rebel politicians of Brunei following the abortive rebellion in December 1962.

Hence, it is no coincidence that the two smallest states in ASEAN have maintained the most cordial relations with one another, their cultural and economic differences notwithstanding. Being small in size and population, Brunei and Singapore feel vulnerable and find common ground to cooperate with each other in many fields, including education and defence. Both are committed strongly to the continuity of the military presence of the Commonwealth-ANZUK powers: Brunei maintains a strong Gurkha contingent of soldiers under British officers, while Singapore supports the continuity of the Five Power Defence Arrangement. There is a mutual defence arrangement between Brunei and Singapore which allows for the training of their armed forces in each other's country. Thus, although ASEAN regionalism is based on the theoretical assumption of the equality of states, in practice, the larger ASEAN states have come to exert greater influence over the regional organization. The discussion of equality of states becomes rhetoric when regional interest is subsumed under individual national interest, which dictates that the ultimate goals of the state be pursued by various means. In the case of Indonesia, the central diplomatic concern is to exert regional leadership. President Sukarno employed aggressive means, while President Suharto resorts to peaceful and diplomatic means.

Economic Cooperation and National Development

Prior to the Bali Summit of February 1976, the ASEAN governments had not given sufficient attention to economic cooperation.[10] Only in its tenth year did the ASEAN governments find the political will to lay down a broad programme of economic cooperation, which became the basis of an official blueprint for the implementation of various projects.[11] Even then, the record has not been impressive.

The broad programme envisages three main strategies to promote economic cooperation: preferential trading arrangements (PTA), joint industrial ventures (JIV) and economic ties with the free market economies, viz., the United States, Japan, the European Community, Australia, New Zealand and Canada. Both the PTA and JIV projects are aimed at intra-ASEAN economic cooperation and the creation of a common economic unit. The PTA[12] project has resulted in the listing of over 10,000 items of goods which would be given preferential treatment, viz., lower tarrif rates when imported by other member states. Observers note that these items are either produced locally or poorly demanded in the other markets. Hence, the short term objective of increasing intra-ASEAN trade has not been achieved. In fact, trade between the ASEAN states and other countries has grown appreciably faster than has the intra-ASEAN trade.

Similarly, the JIV[13] project has not been as successful as it was first thought it could be. At the Bali Summit, each member state offered an industrial project which would be subscribed to by the others. Indonesia and Malaysia opted for urea factories, the Philippines for soda ash, Thailand for phosphate and Singapore the diesel engine project. To date, only the urea factories in Indonesia and Malaysia have been completed. That the expectations from these JIV projects have not been fulfilled, can be explained by several reasons. Firstly, the major investor in these projects is Japan rather than the ASEAN countries. In fact, the latter provided only token participation. Secondly, the urea fertilizer products have not been in demand in the other ASEAN markets. The other agricultural states such as the Philippines and Thailand have their own factories producing fertilizers while Singapore requires them only for re-export.

The expectation that economic cooperation will take off is based on the assumption of a common need and mutual benefit. In reality, the ASEAN states are competing against each other.[14] Each ASEAN state aims to foster its own national development: to provide for economic growth in order to generate employment, better living conditions and higher per capita GNP. ASEAN states which are primarily commodity-based economies compete for similar markets, foreign investment and technical assistance. For example, Indonesia and Malaysia are rubber producing countries and, together with Brunei, are major exporters of oil and gas. Besides, all the member states except Brunei are seeking markets for their manufactured products. In such a situation, it is inevitable that economic competition constitutes the most striking characteristic of the ASEAN economy. Each ASEAN state advocates an open economy and thus its strategy emphasizes foreign investment and competition. These become more intense during a period of economic recession, such as the one that ASEAN states experienced in recent years.

While ASEAN states are not prepared to sacrifice their national development for the sake of economic cooperation, they have worked assiduously in their negotiations with the western industrialised states and Japan. These "dialogue partners" of ASEAN have, for economic and strategic reasons, established rapport with the regional organization. ASEAN states have found it useful to project a united stand on various international economic issues. For example, they protested against the Australian decision to introduce a new civil aviation policy which would hurt such national airlines as the Singapore Airlines. Another example is the ASEAN's joint stand on the proposal to set up a price stabilization scheme (STABEX), which will safeguard the primary commodity-based states from being seriously affected by the fluctuating demands and prices for their products. The ASEAN states have obtained a variety of financial and technical assistance from the dialogue partners. For example, Japan has provided a US$1 billion aid package to ASEAN to promote manpower resource development. Other western countries such as Australia, New Zealand and Canada have provided funds and experts for various projects in ASEAN countries.

Thus, although ASEAN was set up to promote economic cooperation, little has been achieved in this respect. Instead, the practical consideration for promoting national development has undermined the ideal of regionalism. The advocacy of economic cooperation seems laudable as a diplomatic exercise, but in practice, there are too many obstacles which seem insurmountable for cooperation to fulfil the aspiration of the founders of the regional organization.

Cultural Cooperation and National Identity

ASEAN aims to promote cooperation, greater understanding and appreciation of the culture, religion and language of the various ethnic communities of the member states. In fact, culture, religion and language are crucial determinants for both national unity and inter-state relations. Cultural cooperation appears to be a priority consideration for ASEAN since misconceptions amongst member states may distort their perceptions of each other. For example, because of its majority Chinese population, Singapore is seen to be a kind of "Third China". On the other hand, the overwhelming Malay population in Indonesia, Malaysia and the Philippines gives the region a dominantly Islamic complexion. Both the examples are over-simplifications of the very complex cultural landscape in the ASEAN states. Though ASEAN is comprised of multi-racial states, each government has a different approach to nation-building. In fact, the fundamentally different approach of the state of Singapore, while part of the federation of Malaysia, led to severe political strain and conflict with the federal government. This in turn led to the racial riots of July and September 1964 and the eventual expulsion of Singapore from the federation of Malaysia.

Since ASEAN's establishment, numerous activities have been organised to promote cultural cooperation. For example, ASEAN has organised cultural programmes, arts and drama festivals and exchanged educational publications.[15] Nonetheless, there is no serious effort to promote cooperation via manpower exchanges, joint training programmes, academic exchanges and studies.[16] Some ASEAN countries have offered scholarships for technical and tertiary education. These remain rather limited and constrained by the fact that all the ASEAN countries have different educational and administative systems.

ASEAN cultural cooperation in whatever forms may facilitate the practical efforts of nation-building. What is significant is that the nation-building efforts of one state affect the political stability and cohension of the region. For example, the Philippines and Thailand have sizeable Muslim populations which are trying to set up autonomous and even separatist regions in the southern parts of their countries. Another constraint on nation-building is the resurgence of Islamic fundamentalism in Indonesia, Malaysia, the Philippines and Thailand.

Two recent strains in Malaysia-Singapore relations show the importance of cultural and religious factors in ASEAN cooperation. When a Singapore Minister cast doubts on the loyalty of Singapore Malays in the Armed Forces, the Malays across the causeway in Malaysia immediately protested that this represented an attempt to undermine the integrity of the Malay race as a whole. A morc serious example is that of the visit of President Herzog to Singapore. In this case, all of the three Muslim dominated states, viz., Brunei, Indonesia and Malaysia protested vociferously against Singapore's decision. Malaysian leaders were particularly vocal in their protests and demonstrations.

A development which does not augur well for ASEAN's cultural cooperation is the resurgence of Islamic fundamentalism in the Muslim states, particularly in Malaysia. The dominance of Islamic fundamental beliefs on government policies in Malaysia is likely to affect interstate relations in ASEAN. Even Indonesia, which has adopted an accommodative ideology of "Pancasila" for nation-building, is wary of the development of Islamic fundamentalism in Malaysia.

Cultural factors such as race and language also have impact on ASEAN's external relationship with the major powers, especially China. The Singapore government has been consistent in stating that it would have diplomatic relations with China only after the Indonesian government has done so. Such a policy is meant to placate the sensitivity of the Muslim states and to ensure that the nation-building process in Singapore proceeds without undue complications.

Thus, the cultural diversity within and between the ASEAN states has hampered the full realization of the goal of effective regional cooperation. The rhetoric of regional cooperation must contend with the practical problems of nation-building in each ASEAN state.

Security Cooperation and National Policy

ASEAN was founded in the midst of the political and security uncertainties both in relation to intra-regional and to external strategic environments. Though the founding members agreed to normalise their diplomatic relations, the underlying political and security conflicts persisted. Meantime, regional conflicts such as the Vietnam war had intensified. ASEAN cooperation in the political and security fronts was necessary to reduce the bilateral and regional conflicts. While consensus was sought on international issues, national inclinations were not discouraged.

The most persuasive argument for a common stand on international issues is that the ASEAN states, except for Thailand, share relatively similar political experiences of colonialism, imperialism, Japanese occupation, communist subversion and insurrection. Additionally, the geographical location of ASEAN states which straddles the vital sea lanes of the Pacific and Indian Oceans has made the region a strategic area for major global powers. Both because of the historical experiences with external powers and the strategic value of the region, the ASEAN states are anxious to free the region from external intervention.

In August 1971, ASEAN adopted the Kuala Lumpur Declaration which expresses the ASEAN aspiration to set up a zone of peace, freedom and neutrality (ZOPFAN) in Southeast Asia.[17] Some ASEAN members expressed reluctance to participate in ZOPFAN, particularly the Philippines and Thailand which have strong security links with the United States. In reality, so long as the superpowers maintain military bases in the region—the United States in the Philippines and the Soviet Union in Vietnam—ZOPFAN will remain very much in the realm of wishful thinking.

In June 1987, the ASEAN members agreed to explore the possibility of making Southeast Asia a nuclear weapon-free zone (NWFZ). This marked another development of ZOPFAN. The ASEAN formula remains flexible and moderate,[18] approximating that of the Japanese.

Although the ASEAN states have adopted ZOPFAN and are moving towards NWFZ, they are pragmatic enough to realize the imperative of maintaining the balance of power in the Asia-Pacific region. Both the United States and the Soviet Union maintain military bases and facilities in the Philippines and Vietnam respectively. In response to calls for the withdrawal of bases from Cam Ranh Bay and Danang, Moscow has indicated that it will consider this if the Americans were to reciprocate. A re-negiotated Military Bases Agreement between the United States and the Philippines will be the raison d'être for the continuation of the Soviet bases in Vietnam.

ASEAN's support for the US presence in the region is tacit in nature without compromising the non-alignment principles of member states such as Indonesia and Malaysia. Despite the calls by the Philippines for a united ASEAN stand on the issue of US bases in its locality, the ASEAN governments have not been forthcoming.

ASEAN security cooperation was spelt out in the Bali Declaration of February 1976. It maintained that security cooperation should be on a bilateral basis. ASEAN security cooperation takes the form of consultative meetings and visits to the military academies of the member countries.

In the international arena, ASEAN was preoccupied with solving the Cambodian problem[19]. Since the Vietnamese invasion and occupation of Cambodia in December 1978 to January 1979, ASEAN has been very active in mobilizing international opinion against the Vietnamese aggression. ASEAN was successful in obtaining the United Nations' support of its proposal to reach a comprehensive political settlement of the Cambodia problem. The proposal called *inter alia*, for the withdrawal of the Vietnamese troops from Cambodia, the right of self-determination for Cambodians and the establishment of an independent and neutral state in Cambodia. This proposal received a record 117 votes of UN members when it was debated before the United Nations General Assembly (UNGA) in October 1987

ASEAN was also successful in rallying the international community to retain the Cambodian seat in the UN for the Coalition Government of Democratic Kampuchea (CGDK).[20] From 1979 to 1982, the credential issue was hotly debated in the UN. Such debates were put to rest after the CGDK obtained strong support in 1982. It should be noted that not all ASEAN members relish the thought of supporting the CGDK, for its Khmer Rouge faction was responsible for the deaths of about a million Cambodians during April 1975-December 1978.

A more thorny issue concerns the composition of the coalition government, which will replace the Hanoi-controlled Heng Samrin regime. The consensus seems to be that the new government should be headed by Prince Sihanouk. Moreover, Cambodia should not pose a serious threat to its neighbours, whether they be Vietnam or Thailand. Besides, it is felt that Pol Pot and Ieng Sary—the two most notorious leaders of the brutal Khmer Rouge government—should be excluded. The question is under what circumstances can these Khmer Rouge leaders be removed? This implies that consent must be sought from China.

Until then, ASEAN has been active in supporting moves to bring the parties to the conflict to the negotiating table. ASEAN has called on the Soviet Union to exert pressure on Vietnam to agree to talks with Sihanouk, but to no avail. Indonesia and Vietnam agreed in July 1987 to organize a cocktail party to which all four Cambodian factions would be invited in an informal capacity and to meet without pre-conditions or fixed agenda. But this agreement came against the insistence of Thailand that Vietnam must immediately participate in the cocktail party. Eventually, however, agreement was reached by all parties concerned to hold an informal meeting in Bogor, Indonesia in July 1988.

The Geneva accord on the Afghanistan problem gave hope of an early settlement of the Cambodian problem. The Soviet withdrawal of its forces from Afghanistan provided useful lessons for Cambodia. That is, Vietnamese withdrawal from Cambodia would allow the Cambodians to sort out their problems themselves. However, in view of the fear of the return of the Khmer Rouge, which is not in the interests of any power except China, there would have to be an international guarantee that the right of self-determination for the Cambodians could be exercised. Thus, the Cambodian problem could be solved in a Geneva-type meeting, albeit with firmer guarantees by an international organisation such as the UN[21] of sanctions against violations of regional order.

Thus, we see that on the question of security cooperation, ASEAN has achieved far more than in the other areas. This can be explained by several main factors including the common concern about internal security by the ASEAN states, vigilance against external intervention and the flexibility with which member states pursue their national policies. Such common interests and flexibility will ensure that ASEAN's unity and cohesion in the international environment will be strengthened in the years ahead.

Ideology and Regional Cooperation

To what extent has the ideological factor, specifically the question of anti-communism,[22] been a key determinant of ASEAN cooperation? All the ASEAN governments have declared communism illegal and even opposed the free dissemination of Marxist literature. The total ban of communism is a result of many years of struggle between the communist parties and the non-communist governments. With the British help, Brunei overcame a socialist and communist-assisted rebellion in December 1962. Indonesia also experienced an abortive coup by the Indonesian Communist Party in September 1965, while Malaysia and Singapore survived the communist insurgencies of 1948-1960. Similarly, the Philippines government defeated the communists in the 1950s and Thailand has largely contained the communists' threat since the late 1970s. These events are the key benchmarks of the ongoing struggle between the non-communist governments and the communists in the ASEAN region. All of them face the constant threat from the communist party either through covert or overt actions. Hence, there is a common basis for the ASEAN governments to ensure that the indigenous communist movement does not succeed in any ASEAN country.[23]

All the ASEAN countries believe that the main thrust against the communists lies in economic growth, equitable distribution of wealth and a higher standard of living. For these to be possible, there must be political stability and laissez-faire conditions to attract the foreign capital, expertise and manpower of the industrialised countries. Political stability demands, above all, the elimination of the communists from the politics of the land. To achieve this gaol, constant and extensive cooperation amongst the ASEAN governments is necessary.

The ASEAN governments have cooperated to fight against the communist insurgents who operate across the borders. Thus, Malaysia and Thailand have an active and comprehensive programme to wipe out the remnants of the MCP which occupy the southern territories of Thailand. Similarly, the Indonesian and Malaysian governments conduct joint border operations in Sarawak and Kalimantan. Between Malaysia and Singapore there are constant and regular exchanges of information pertaining to communist subversion and infiltration into social and political organizations.

While the ASEAN governments are uncompromising as far as communism in their own countries is concerned, they are prepared to establish diplomatic ties with foreign communist governments on the basis of peaceful co-existence. Thus, most of the ASEAN governments have diplomatic relations with China, the Soviet Union and other East European countries. Most of them have dealings with Laos and Vietnam but none has recognised the Heng Samrin regime. Both Indonesia and Singapore have no diplomatic relations with China. And Indonesia will only normalise relations with China if Beijing agrees not to interfere in the former's internal affairs and to sever ties with the Indonesian Communist Party.

Generally, the ASEAN governments tend to favour the United States and the West in their foreign policy orientation.[24] Although some of the ASEAN states declare themselves to be non-aligned, they have very close ties with the United States and the West. Undoubtedly, their security and economic growth are linked to the Western industrial countries and Japan. The Philippines and Thailand are directly linked to the United States through bilateral treaties and the Manila Pact. Malaysia and Singapore are indirectly linked by the Five-Power Defence Arrangement. All the ASEAN countries except Brunei receive American military support either in the form of military aid or concessionary purchase. All the ASEAN states have agreed that a balance of power situation is necessary to maintain peace and stability in the Asia-Pacific region. This means that they will continue to back the American military presence in the Philippines to balance the Soviet presence in Cam Ranh Bay and Danang.

Whether or not the orientation of a western-inclined ASEAN will remain will depend on the successive leadership. There is a likelihood of leadership continuity for all the ASEAN states except the Philippines. In Brunei, there is a young ruler and the slow political reforms are unlikely to endanger his supremacy. In Indonesia and Thailand, new and powerful politicians backed by military leaders are going to succeed the military-dominated political systems. In Singapore, the new generation of leaders is ready to take over the government without causing any serious political strife. In Malaysia, the succession issue had been clouded by the rift among the Malays. But there is no doubt that the Malay leadership will continue to dominate politics in Malaysia. Only in the Philippines has the issue of leadership succession posed serious problems and significiant implications for the ASEAN and Asia-Pacific regions. If the new generation decides to severe the longstanding ties with the United States, the rest of ASEAN may have to review the security options available in order for the regional organisation to remain intact.

Conclusion

In the ultimate analysis, the historical and political factors have been the dominant determinants of the ASEAN diplomacy and practice. Years under western imperialism, Japanese occupation and communist rebellion have conditioned the ASEAN governments and their peoples to be cautious in their dealings with external powers. Moreover, the lessons of dependence on external powers have not been forgotten by the ASEAN leaders. External powers have to serve their own national interests and their political constituents, hence, their foreign policies are merely expedient measures subject to changes in leadership and political climate. This is particularly so for the western liberal countries.

ASEAN seeks to achieve regional resilience. This means, *inter alia*, intra-ASEAN cooperation to achieve greater political stability, social cohesion, domestic economic growth and regional order as well as flexible relationships with foreign powers. The record of ASEAN development since its formation in 1967 shows how successful ASEAN has been in achieving these goals.

ASEAN diplomacy has not been achieved at the expense of the national interests of individual states. With the exception of the Philippines, all have managed to maintain political stability. Although inter-ethnic rivalries and communist subversions still constitute threats to regional stability, it appears unlikely that established political institutions will be dismantled in the immediate future. Economically, the impressive growth rates of the ASEAN states speak for themselves. ASEAN has indeed been regarded as the success story of the Third World.

ASEAN continues to explore the development of ZOPFAN and to seek the settlement of the Cambodian problem. Although member states differ slightly in their approaches to contain regional conflicts, ASEAN has maintained a joint front against the Vietnamese occupation of Cambodia. Such a concerted action has even accommodated Indonesia's effort to persuade the Vietnamese to negotiate. This has not weakened ASEAN's unity and cooperation in any way.

Internationally, ASEAN is regarded as a united organisation and increasingly the dialogue partners are treating ASEAN as a regional bloc. Even the Soviet Union, China and Vietnam have now recognised ASEAN as a regional organisation.

ASEAN's success can be attributed to certain *modus operandi* and it may become a model for other Third World regional organisations. These principles include unity in diversity, consensual decision-making, and common agreement on regional order and unification. Nonetheless, the independence and sovereignty of ASEAN states are respected in that their national interests are considered when the organisation makes collective decisions. Moreover, the tacit acceptance of intra-ASEAN diversities has contributed to the solidarity of ASEAN. Consensus is often arrived at through patient and informal consultations amongst the Heads of member states. In the final analysis, however, it is the political will of the ASEAN leaders which has made ASEAN what it is today.

NOTES

1 ''Reflections on Promoting Aseanism'', *Sin Chew Jit Poh Sunday Edition*, 27 August 1987 reprinted in *Economics and Current Affairs. Volume I*, Sin Chew Jit Poh 1978, pp. 21-29; Hans H. Indorf, *Impediments to Regionalism in Southeast Asia*, ASEAN Political Studies, Institute of Southeast Asian Studies, 1984, pp. 1-3. Chua Hian Kong, Robert, *ASEAN: Problems and Prospects for Integration*, Department of Political Science, University of Singapore, 1978/79, Chapters 2-3.

2 M. Rajendran, *ASEAN's Foreign Relations—The Shift to Collective Action*, Arenabuku Sdn Bhd, Kuala LUmpur, 1985, pp. 208-211.

3 As Mr. S. Rajaratnam pointed out, the major challenge for ASEAN is to ''marry national thinking to regional thinking''. See Levi Werner, *The Challenge of World Politics in South and Southeast Asia,* New Jersey: Prentice-Hall Inc., 1968, p. 67.

4 See Arnfinn Jorgensen-Dahl, *Regional Organisation and Order in Southeast Asia*, St Martin's Press, New York 1982, pp. 9-64; Hans H. Indorf, *op. cit.*, pp. 5-10.

5 Chua Hian Kong, Robert, *op. cit.*, pp. 25-29.

6 Arnfinn Jorgensen-Dahl, *op. cit.*, pp. 30-32.

7 *Ibid.*, pp. 33-34.

8 For a discussion of the Indonesian perception of threats to Southeast Asian Security, see Juwono Sudarsono, ''Security in Southeast Asia: The Circle of Conflict'', in Robert A. Scalapino and Jusuf Wanandi, *Economic, Political and Security Issues in Southeast Asia in the 1980s*, University of California, USA, 1982, pp. 63-68.

9 Hans H. Indorf, *op. cit.*, pp. 42-46.

10 Indeed, there was no decision reached in Bali that a regular summit be held to promote regional economic cooperation. See ''Reflections on Promoting Aseanism'', *Economics and Current Affairs, op. cit.*

11 *ASEAN: The Way Forward—The Report of the Group of Fourteen on ASEAN Economic Cooperation and Integration*, Institute of Strategic and International Studies (ISIS), Malaysia, Kuala Lumpur, 1987, pp. 3-87. Opening Statement by Prime Minister Lee Kuan Yew in the *Meetings of the ASEAN Heads of Government, Manila, 17-15 December 1987 and Meeting of the ASEAN Heads of Government and the Prime Minister of Japan. Manila 15 December 1987,* pp. 20-21: *Annual Report of the ASEAN Standing Committee 1985-1986*, ASEAN Secretariat, Indonesia, pp. 7-9 and pp. 56-57.

13 ''ASEAN Industrial Projects—the need for a Caesarean Operation'', *Sin Chew Jit Poh*, September 17, 1978 reprinted in *Economics and Current Affairs, op. cit.*, pp. 48-47; Opening Statement by Mr S. Dhanabalan in *19th ASEAN Ministerial Meetings and Post Ministerial Conferences with the Dialogue Partners*, Manila 23-28 June 1968, ASEAN Secretariat, Indonesia, p. 13; *ASEAN: The Way Forward, ibid.*, pp. 31-37.

14 Robert A. Scalapino, Seizaburo Sato and Jusuf Wanandi (ed.), *Asian Economic Development—Present and Future*, Institute of East Asian Studies, University of California, 1985, pp. 161-192 and pp. 216-238; Lee Soo Ann (ed.), *Economic Problems and Prospects in ASEAN Countries*, Applied Research Corporation, Singapore 1977, pp. 163-170.

15 *Annual Report of the ASEAN Standing Committee*, 1985-86, *op. cit.*, pp. 88-97.

16 As Professor Lim Chong Yah argued, to have ballast, ASEAN should also be a social and educational grouping. This can be done via more exchanges of students, artists and

scholars amongst the ASEAN states. ASEAN cooperation should also be supported by what is equivalent to an ASEAN Colombo Plan. See "Reflections on Aseanism", *Economics and Current Affairs, op. cit.*

17 Robert O. Tilman, *The Enemy Beyond, External Threat Perceptions in the ASEAN Region*, Institute of Southeast Asian Studies, Research Notes and Discussion Paper No. 42, 1984, pp. 10-12; Robert Scalapino, Seizaburo Sato and Jusuf Wanandi (ed.), *Internal and External Security Issues in Asia*, Institute of East Asian Studies, University of California 1986, p. 174; See Chua Hian·Kong, Robert, *op. cit.*, pp. 63-65.

18 *20th ASEAN Ministerial Meetings and Post-Ministerial Conferences with the Dialogue Partners, op. cit.*, especially p. 21, pp. 28-31, pp. 38-39, p. 50, pp. 68-71, pp. 82-84 and pp. 119-121.

19 According to Prime Minister Lee Kuan Yew, the Cambodian issue crucially decided "the balance of forces between the communist group of countries and the non-communist group of countries" See "My view by the Prime Minister", *Straits Times*, 12 October 1984, p. 11 and "ASEAN Summit: Leaders Fly in", *Straits Times*, 14 December 1987, p. 1.

20 *20th ASEAN Ministerial Meeting and Post-Ministerial Conferences with the Dialogue Partners, op. cit.*, pp. 20-21, pp. 48-49 and pp. 72-73.

21 Robert A. Scalapino, Seizaburo Sato and Jusuf Wanandi, *op. cit.*, pp. 239-243; Arnfinn Jorgensen-Dahl, *op. cit.*, pp. 92-99.

22 The formation of ASEAN was a response "by the non-communist Southeast Asia to the western abandonment of its role as a shield against communism". See S. Rajaratnam, "ASEAN demonstrates working system" in *Speeches*, Ministry of Culture, Volume I, No. 5, November 1977, Singapore.

23 Donald E. Weatherbee, "The Indigenization of ASEAN Communist Parties", in Charles E. Morrison (ed.), *Threats in East Asia-Pacific—National and Regional Perspectives*, Lexington Books, D. C. Heath and Company, Singapore, 1983, pp. 161-185.

24 Robert A. Scalapino, Seizaburo Sato and Jusuf Wanandi, 1986, *op. cit.*, pp. 26-43 and pp. 246-273.

CONTRIBUTORS

Dr. Robert E. Bedeski received his PH.D. from the University of California at Berkeley in 1969. He has taught at Ohio State University and at the National Defence College in Tokyo. His articles and essays have been published in *World Politics, China Quarterley, Asian Survey, International Perspectives, Etudes Internationale, Electoral Studies* and other journals. He has pursued field research in the People's Republic of China, Japan, The Republic of Korea, Taiwan, and Hong Kong. His major publications include *State-Building in Modern China: The Kuomintang in the Prewar Period.* (Berkeley: University of California, Institute of East Asian Studies, 1981.); *The Fragile Entente: The 1978 Japan-China Peace Treaty in a Global Context.* (Boulder, CO: Westview Press, 1983.); and *The People's Republic of China-Relations in Asia: The Strategic Implications.* (Ottawa: Department of National Defence, Operational Research and Analysis Establishment, ORAE Extra-Mural Paper No. 32, 1984) *South Korea's Modernization: Confucian and Conservative Characteristics.* (Working Paper #21, "Canada and the Pacific: Agenda for the Eighties", The Joint Centre on Modern Wast Asia, University of Toronto, 1984); and *Japan's Defence Policy and its Strategic Implications.* (Ottawa: Department of National Defence, Operational Research and Analysis Establishment, ORAE Extra-Mural Paper, 1985).

Ashok Kapur (Ph.D., Carleton University, 1974) is Professor of Political Science, University of Waterloo, Ontario, Canada. He is the author of *India's Nuclear Option* (1976), *International Nuclear Proliferation* (1979), *The Indian Ocean* (1983), *Pakistan's Nuclear Development* (1987) and scholarly articles on Indian Foreign Policy.

Dr. Rezun has written extensively on Soviet-Middle Eastern affairs; his major work, *The Soviet Union and Iran* (1981), has been called a classic and has been reprinted by Westview (1988). He has written other books in both English and Russian, including numerous articles in French. His current area of research and writing has focused on Soviet reform and computerization; a book entitled *Reform, Science and Technology Under Gorbachev* is due to appear in 1991. He is Associate Professor in Political Science at the University of New Brunswick in Fredericton, Canada.

Professor Shen Shouyuan joined the Chinese foreign service in 1954 on graduation from the English Department of the Beijing Foreign Languages Institute, predecessor of the present Beijing Foreign Studies University. He was a visiting scholar at the School of Advanced International Studies (SAIS) of the Johns Hopkins University, Washington, D.C., U.S.A., for a year (1985-86) doing researches in international relations; his paper "Sino-European Relations in the Global Context: Increased Parallels in an Increasingly Plural World" was published in *Asian Survey*, Vol. XXVI, No. 11, November 1986, University of California Press, Berkeley. He is now on the faculty of the Foreign Affairs College in Beijing.

Lau Teik Soon obtained the degrees of BA Honours (First Class), University of Singapore in 1966, and the Ph.D., (International Relations) Australia National University in 1972. Soon after, he joined the Department of Political Science. Presently, he is the Head of the Department. His area of specialism is the international politics of the Asia-Pacific region, and he has taught international relations courses including international politics of Southeast Asia and strategic and regional security issues. He has published numerous articles and edited books on various political and international issues pertaining to the Asia-Pacific region.

Associate Professor Huan Zhongging was also recruited in the foreign service after completing her studies as a major in English at the Beijing Foreign Languages Institute in 1963. She undertook a two-year research programme in international relations at Queen Elizabeth House, Oxford University, the United Kingdom, from 1983-1985. She gives lectures on strategic aspects of international politics at the Foreign Affairs in Beijing, and has published a number of papers in Chinese academic journals.

Russell B. Trood teaches at Griffith University, Brisbane, Australia. He has lectured on related topics at the Australian Joint Services Staff College and the RAAF Staff College, and is the author of various articles and chapters in books on security and foreign policy issues. He is as co-editor and contributor to *The Indian Ocean: Perspectives on Strategic Arena*, published by Duke University Press in 1985.

A. J. Wilson, Ph.D., D. Sc. (Econ.) London, taught at the University of Ceylon (1952-72) and was Founding Chair and head of Department of Economics and Political Science when he joined the University of New Brunswick (1972-). He is the author of several works: *Politics in Sri Lanka* (1974 and 1979); *Electoral Politics in an Emergent State* (1975); *The Gaullist System in Asia: The Constitution of Sri-Lanka, 1978* (1980); *The Breakup of Sri Lanka* (1988); and co-editor with Denis Dalton of *The States of South Asia: Problem of National Integration* (1982), among other works. He was also the intermediary between President J. R. Jayewardene and the Tamil United Liberation Front during 1978-83. He has held visiting appointments at the universities of Leicester, Oxford, Manchester, McGill and Columbia.

INDEX